From Street Smart to School Smart

Also by Dr. David P. Sortino

Brain Changers: Major Advances in Children's Learning and Intelligence

A Guide to How Your Child Learns: Understanding the Brain from Infancy to Young Adulthood

Brain Gains: Major Advances in Children's Learning and Intelligence

The Promised Cookie: No Longer Angry Children

From Street Smart to School Smart

The Unmaking of the Sisters of the Streets

Inspired by a true story

David P. Sortino

ROWMAN & LITTLEFIELD
Lanham • Boulder • New York • London

Published by Rowman & Littlefield
An imprint of The Rowman & Littlefield Publishing Group, Inc.
4501 Forbes Boulevard, Suite 200, Lanham, Maryland 20706
www.rowman.com

British Library Cataloguing in Publication Information Available

Library of Congress Cataloging-in-Publication Data

Names: Sortino, David P., author.
Title: From street smart to school smart : the unmaking of a street walker / David P. Sortino.
Description: Lanham, Maryland : Rowman & Littlefield Publishers, [2021] | "Inspired by a true story"--Title page. | Summary: "This fictional story about 17-year-old Jewels Odom and 13 other ex-teen prostitutes gives Jewels and her 13 "sisters" a pulpit to speak to other lost girls looking for an escape from what they call the "streets of hell." What separates Jewels from her "street sisters" is her ability to survive and succeed -- actually going to college to return as a teacher at juvie. This story ends with a mixture of successes and failures, but as always, Jewels is the one who has the final say when she tries to connect with Maya Angelou, the famous poet, to be the graduation speaker"-- Provided by publisher.
Identifiers: LCCN 2021014366 (print) | LCCN 2021014367 (ebook) | ISBN 9781475861105 (paperback) | ISBN 9781475861129 (epub)
Subjects: LCSH: Prostitutes. | Self-actualization (Psychology)
Classification: LCC HQ118 .S68 2021 (print) | LCC HQ118 (ebook) | DDC 306.74--dc23
LC record available at https://lccn.loc.gov/2021014366
LC ebook record available at https://lccn.loc.gov/2021014367

"There is no greater agony than bearing an untold story inside you!"

—Maya Angelou

Contents

Author's Note

The genesis of my book, *From Street Smart to School Smart*, was initiated some years ago. I was a college freshman in a child development class when my instructor's "stinging" statement caused a near explosion in my brain, revealing to me the cause of my serious acting-out behavior as a third grader, which had been out of control.

He explained almost flippantly that "eight-year-old children can comprehend that when a person's dies, they do not return! You are kaput! However, prior to age 8, children's perception of death is less permanent—that is, when individuals die, they could return someday."

In my third-grade year, two major events had occurred that would inspire my acting-out behavior and this definitive reaction to death. First, my grandfather, a beacon of strength in my Italian American family, passed away. Secondly, my father was offered a promotion at a large corporation in Los Angeles, which meant that he would fly frequently from the East Coast to the West Coast for interviews. When I overheard my mother speak about one such trip during which my father's flight had made an emergency landing, I had felt a panic in my chest.

Thereafter, I began acting out in school, resulting in numerous trips to the hallway or principal. The moral of the story is that I realized my father could die in a plane crash; I thought I could keep him from flying to the West Coast if I became a serious behavior problem. Fortunately, he didn't take the job, but for years, my third-grade behavior stuck in my body like a virus until that eventful child development class. I felt an almost immediate connection with my entire painful third-grade experience, motivating me to major in psychology so I could become a vehicle to a better understanding of children's behaviors. I eventually graduated with a degree in psychology and a special education teaching credential, which offered me a path to work with at-risk children and youth at a bankrupt state regional school called Project RESCUE (Regional Educational Services in Unified Education).

After two teachers at this school resigned, it was assumed I would follow the path the students had previously demanded: "Teach us something we can use in real life!" With the permission of the school's director, I changed the school's curriculum and created a program that attempted to empower at-risk adolescents. For example, I individualized the academic curriculum—allowing all students to work on their own academic level—as well as creating work-study positions in stores, libraries, and farms to enhance responsibility and social interaction with the adults who managed them.

Also, I developed an afternoon arts program that allowed students to select what activities stimulated their interests best! This sense of empowerment changed the students' perception and respect of rules. By the end of the school year, 75 percent of our at-risk youth returned to their home schools. Our success doubled the enrollment size as well as provided much-needed money for our school to survive bankruptcy. In fact, RESCUE's success inspired me to write a book about this successful teaching experience called *The Promised Cookie—No Longer Angry Children* (Author House, 2011). The three-year Project RESCUE experience motivated me to apply to Harvard University, leading to study with my advisor, the late Dr. Lawrence Kohlberg of the Harvard Center for Moral Education. Dr. Kohlberg had recognized the power of my book and its connection to his moral development theory. Furthermore, my Harvard studies solidified my knowledge and experience to work with at-risk youth.

After Harvard, I was hired as the school principal at a Just Community Emancipation Program for ex-juvenile offenders, ages sixteen to nineteen, called the Clark Academy, the basis and site of this book!

The Clark Academy and the Just Community approach to at-risk youth is designed to give the power of rules and laws to inmates by helping them create the rules and consequences for their school or residential living units, or Just Community. At the beginning of the school year, all staff and students participate in what is called a Constitutional Convention to create the rules and consequences for their school and residential living area. Through the Constitutional Convention, a rule book or manual is created. Each Friday two students and one staff member meet with student rule violators to receive their discipline from the Just Community rule book. The main purpose of the Just Community Program is to expose repeat lawbreakers to the power of the law by giving them a say in the rules of their school and living unit. Finally, it is hoped that the Just Community theory will carry over to when they leave the Clark Academy and return to a society governed by rules and laws.

Throughout my three years as the school's principal, I incorporated much of my success from Project RESCUE with a philosophy that sought to empower the Clark Academy students by giving them the opportunity to help build their own school or classroom. In order to achieve this goal, I needed to personalize the experience by taking trips to lumberyards to buy materials for their new classroom, to warehouses in San Francisco to buy used desks, and trips to a book repository to buy their schoolbooks. The simple act of personalizing such empowering experiences reinforced Dr. Kohlberg's theories on reciprocity, conformity, and respect for law and order.

The silver lining to such an experience meant that in our sojourns to various destinations off of school grounds, the girls chose not to be tempted to return to the always-lurking ex-pimps, drug dealers, and gang bangers who yet tried to lure the girls back into their realms, a realm the girls described as governed by the "man on the floor." They were choosing new values. What had happened with the "men on the floor" and the girls was that once the girls realized the importance of their school program, they discontinued their sexual innuendos, and the new "men on the floor" responded with the seriousness and concern of healthy male mentors. I chose one particular student, Jewels Odom, as the main character in this book, serving as the voice and/or commentary to represent the girls and their program. Although Jewels's name is fictional, her character a melding of two girls in the program, and 90 percent of my story is true.

After I left the Clark Academy, I obtained a PhD in clinical psychology and worked at a North Bay juvenile hall for four years as a moral development consultant, running groups and retraining staff about recent developmental theories, and so on. In addition to my work at the hall, I also taught several university courses in moral development and the life cycle. I also wrote a blog for the *Santa Rosa Press Democrat* to support my work and experience with at-risk youth. Readers can go to the *Santa Rosa Press Democrat* for a list of my articles. Finally, over the past three years I have published three books to support my personal experience as a teacher and parent of my own two beautiful daughters, Shai and Abby Sortino. The following book only adds to my experience and knowledge of at-risk youth and children. Currently I work with adolescents as a neurofeedback provider, hoping to provide another pathway to improving the human learning experience.

Moreover, my career experiences and studies in psychology, moral developmental education, and brain development have given me the tools as an expert in the field regarding the development of moral judgment. My methods have increased positive school performance with at-risk youth. This publication is the end result of my journey, compressed into one powerful story.

David P. Sortino, EdM, PhD

Preface

Dear Reader:

The dominant theme of *From Street Smart to School Smart: The Unmaking of Sisters of the Streets* emerges from the sound of a man or woman yelling, "man on the floor," a warning call to girls that had to deal, in their earlier experiences, with various threatening or structured environments, including juvenile hall, jail, residential treatment programs, group homes, and even foster homes.

In short, the phrase, "man on the floor" phrase should never be confused with the men on the streets who had previously dominated their lives and essentially used them and held them captive until they were arrested and sent to one of the above treatment facilities.

For example, males such as their fathers who deserted them; the pimps who exploited and beat them; the gang bangers who forced them to commit crimes and fight; the drug dealers who got them hooked on crack; the "Johns" who took their dignity; however, it was the overlap of a controlled environment, run by men, that was being used for rehabilitation but was also yet, very close to "man on the street." How was a vulnerable abused young woman to learn to trust a man in a controlled environment after the "men on the street? And that is the miracle transformation that occurs is this account entitled, "Man on the Floor."

The reader learns from the girls' own lips that many males in such facilities only reinforced indignities once experienced on the street. Many of these men were staff members who confined them in humiliating circumstances; residential treatment staff often considered them to be mentally ill. Even our two Harvard PhD directors, in their attempt to create a program based on moral development theory, struggled in their understanding of the "Man on the Floor" dilemma that had dominated the lives of their fourteen juvenile offender girls. In a word, what was absent from the Clark Academy Just Community Program and where our story takes place was the understanding that the fourteen juvenile offender females chosen for the program needed not only an academic training and identity, but also deep emotional rehabilitation in areas of trust of authority figures and intimate relationships with any other person, in order to pass the GED (Graduate Educational Development) exam. Although their dignity had been stolen from them on the Oakland/San Francisco streets and in and several rehabilitation environments, their experiences had also given them a street smart personality, a strength that would allow them to function in a world that was based purely on survival. Nevertheless, these girls needed to see that learning and intelligence need not be purely academic as in math or English, but also in the form of emotional intelligence that would allow them to survive in a very challenging world. When I appeared for my interview at the school run by the two Harvard PhD directors, it was advertised that the candidates for the school director's position would be a part of an innovative experimental program called "The Just Community" for juvenile offenders that could also help them pass the GED or the Graduate Record Examination. (The Just Community was modeled after the Connecticut prison riots that forced the warden to enlist the Harvard Center for Moral Education to consult with staff to start a Just Community. In that program, the inmates made the rules or laws and consequences for their living unit.)

Since I had graduated from the same Harvard University program as our two executive directors, I was excited that we could create a program that would transcend other programs for at risk youth or, in our case, females who were ex–juvenile offenders. However, I had fallen into the same trap as the two former directors. What was actually needed was not only the academic or a moral development program, but also a school program that combined their street smarts with their school smarts. Unless this was achieved, I would only become another "Man on the Floor" they could not be trusted, and I would fail.

Throughout this experience, I periodically introduced them to males who were not only street smart, but also respectful of them for being intelligent human beings, who would not see them only for their bodies with promiscuous sexual pasts. I took them out of their street smart world and brought them into a world that nurtured trust and respect for human beings, not valued only as seductive items of property. I had to become the new "man on the floor," a man that wished for their well-being and success in life as valued human beings.

For instance, when I walked into the school mansion for my interview, my first encounter was with a drugged out teen who simply asked me if I had a smoke. When I politely said, "I do not smoke," she responded angrily, "Then what are you good for, honkie man?!" Close by were three other teenage girls fighting over who would get to use the pay phone first! Scattered around the school were girls lying on the floor, curled up in blankets, and others sleeping on couches. The school classroom was filled with discarded junk. I asked one of the line counselors about the school schedule, and she responded, "Everything is individualized. The girls come and go whenever they finish their schoolwork."

My interview was a scatter shot of questions met by multiple student interruptions, girls asking for more money for laundry, weekend passes, and so on. If I were ever to be hired as the school director, I would have to eliminate any illusion I had about the current school's so called pseudo academic philosophy and take it upon myself to find a way to convince the students, directors, and myself that a purely academic/moral connection would only fail the girls. We had to integrate their survival skills of the street with their survival skills in the academic and socially accepted realms of the world. When I appeared for my demonstration lesson with three grocery bags filled with the ingredients to make homemade pizza, I was met with anger and disillusionment by the girls. "How are we goin' to pass the GED with a pizza 'man on the floor' teacher?"

Learning how to make pizza required reading the directions and measuring the ingredients, which included math concepts such as fractions and the number of calories in a slice of pizza. It was my hope that this approach would change their perception of learning or school intelligence and would transform their street smarts to school smarts, and help them realize that I was not just another "man on the floor," but someone who was going to show them that true intelligence exists in everyone.

In addition to cooking the pizza, for emotional effect, I brought card tables, red and white checkered Italian tablecloths, and candles in Chianti wine bottles, and I even played Dean Martin music, which to my surprise motivated the girls to do a group sing to the song "That's Amore"! To be brief, my demonstration pizza lesson was a success. I had included the emotional element with the academic element, bringing in the power of teamwork also.

I was hired and my next teaching lesson was for the girls to help me build their classroom. First, I had to take fourteen street smart girls on a field trip to a local lumber yard to buy materials to build their classroom. The girls didn't disappoint and appeared in their street walking clothes.

And when they appeared at the lumber yard, the "man on the floor" appeared in great numbers, viewing the girls dressed like hookers as a good diversion from a boring work day. They came out of the woodwork to help.

However, once they noticed these sexually provocative girls actually becoming interested in learning how to saw, hammer, and stain wood, the workers picked up on the girls' interest and the energy changed from "man, on the floor" as a sexual predator to simply teacher; the men treated the girls with respect. The change in the girls' street smart behavior was noticed immediately when, on our way back to their school, I stopped at a light in front of a large high school at dismissal time. Instead of the girls flipping off the nerds in front of the school, they waved and actually made eye contact. Later, I was told by one of the girls that it was the first time the girls ever felt comfortable in front of regular school students.

The directors saw the change in the girls' perception of their skills and how they were becoming able to blend their survival street intelligence with their new and slowly acquired school intelligence. This transformation was due to a respect for rules that they had helped establish, a principal aspect of the Just Community Program and also due to a new definition of "man on the floor." Developing trust and safe environment was obviously a major factor in allowing success in academic intelligence and of course, emotional intelligence.

The following story is a true account of my one-year's experience helping juvenile offender girls move from a "street smart world to a school smart world."

Acknowledgments

I wish to acknowledge the following individuals who helped bring my story to completion.

First and foremost, Mrs. Jan Corbett, whose unwavering support provided me with the impetus to write this book. Also, Mr. Fred Fuchs, who motivated me to believe that this true story about at-risk teens should be told. My loving wife, Jennifer, and my two daughters, Abby and Shai, who respected my need to complete this story, however long it may have taken. Sally Briggs, whose relentless pursuit of perfection contributed the wonderful image for our front cover. And thanks to Mr. Tom Koerner and Carlie Wall, who believed a story about at-risk youth needed be told. Lastly, to the 900,000 girls, ages ten and older, who are sexually exploited daily throughout America cites.

ONE

The Worst Part of the Game!

Amid the cold, dark silence of an Oakland, California, night, a black Lexus sedan sat alone in an Oakland city back alley. There was a loud grunt, then a long groan; the car shook and a loud sigh could be heard as the passenger side door quickly opened. One high-heeled black leather boot stepped angrily out of the car and then another black boot. Jewels Odom, a strikingly tall, eighteen-year-old black female with long, black hair climbed quickly out of the car. She was all hands and fingers as she tried to fix her disheveled hair. Next, she pulled at her tight, black leather slacks, buttoned her tight, white sweater, and nervously counted a wad of bills.

Jewels screamed, "Pencil dick, you're short twenty!"

Jewels began to count the money again.

A male's voice rang out loudly, "Fuck you, bitch!"

When Jewels grabbed for the car's front door handle, she heard the car doors lock and a loud squeal of laughter. Finally, the black Lexus sedan sped out of the alley, nearly side-swiping a nearby building.

Jewels chased after the car but tripped and fell to the ground. She lay on the ground for a few moments, not moving, until she raised her head slowly and stared off into the black, cold, foggy Oakland night. Her body language penetrated the dark, deserted alley and a feeling of emptiness filled her body. For a few seconds, she began to hyperventilate, as she tried to catch her breath, but the cold air only burned her lungs, causing her to cough.

1

Slowly she picked herself up, wiped dirt off her tight, black leather slacks, and began walking aimlessly in circles. She banged her fists against her thighs in frustration and screamed, "Fuck . . . fuck . . . what do I do now? Latrell is going to beat the living shit out of me if I don't come up with the money!"

Jewels moved out to the busy Oakland city street scene of white noise, hyped-up human beings, and speeding cars. When a speeding car honked at Jewels and slowed down, she stuck her behind out to show her tight, shapely body, but the car only sped off with Jewels slapping her ass at the car in disgust.

Sitting down on the curb, she rubbed her eyes and then sighed. Next, she took off her black spiked high-heel boots and began rubbing her feet like some waitress who had been working a ten-hour restaurant shift. She fumbled for a cigarette pack in her brassiere, pulled out a pack of cigarettes, and then with her lips tried to pull out a cigarette, while still searching for a pack of matches in her black leather purse. She fumbled for the matches, then dropped her purse to the ground, became frustrated, and angrily spit the cigarette out of her mouth. An older black hooker named Wanda, around thirty years of age, who looked about fifty, appeared in the darkness.

Her teased colored blonde hair stuck up high like a bird's nest and her face was caked with pink make-up that only accentuated her tired thirty-something-year-old eyes. Her black, leopard-colored tight slacks were coffee stained, and her black halter top was torn. She could barely drag herself up the sidewalk.

Wanda eyed Jewels and spoke in a surly, slow, voice and asking: "Aren't you a little young to be struttin' your skinny little ass on my turf? You know I'm the only real game in town, bitch!"

Jewels replied with attitude, "I'm not little, I'm not skinny, and I'm not young. I just need to eat! I ain't playin' no games, grandma!"

Wanda pulled back and flashed a sympathetic smile, took out a cigarette pack from her side pocket, and offered Jewels a cigarette. Quickly, Jewels grabbed the cigarette as Wanda looked to find a lighter and then lit the cigarette for Jewels.

Jewels nodded in approval and then took a long, slow drag; she closed her eyes and smiled, as a state of blissful contentment covered her tired face.

Wanda asked, "Bitch, you new here? You got a daddy, I hope?"

Jewels ignored Wanda and kept her focus on smoking and on the many cars speeding along the busy street, until one car screeched to a halt and blasted its horn, startling Jewels from her moment of bliss.

Jewels opened her eyes and stretched her body like a cat stretching from a quiet nap. She turned to Wanda and yelled, "Fuckin' asshole, Latrell is here!" Jewels lowered her voice and whispered, "I can smell that cheap cologne a mile away. He's such a fuckin' low life!"

Wanda, ignored the intrusive car and said, "Girlie girl, you better watch you back with that n****r. That gorilla ain't no good!"

They high-fived each other, and then Jewels walked slowly to where Latrell was waiting in his clean, shiny, black Suburban. Latrell lowered the car door window, revealing a stocky thirtyish black male sitting slumped down behind the wheel. His short hair was slicked back. He wore dark glasses, a bright purple shirt, and around his neck hung several gold chains. Jewels anxiously removed a wad of bills from inside her brassiere, peeled off $200 in twenties, and quickly handed the wad of bills to Latrell.

Latrell grabbed the money and began to carefully count the bills. He took a deep breath, slammed his hand down hard on the steering wheel, and yelled, "Bitch, Latrell got a major problem . . . oh yea, a major fuckin' problem!"

Latrell looked away with a disgusted look, smiled, and said, "Latrell don't like gettin' squeezed. Only $200 bucks?" He raised his voice again. "You ain't squeezin' me now girl, cuz, that will really piss Latrell off and Latrell doesn't like gettin' pissed off!"

Jewels pleaded, "It's been slow, really fuckin' slow. I've been smellin' blue [police] all night. I swear I've been smellin' blue. I'll try to do better."

"I've been out here for over a fuckin' hour and I only smell bullshit!" He continued in a more controlled voice, "I will be back in two hours and you best better have the rest of my money. Remember, Latrell don't play!"

Latrell rolled up the side window, paused, then rolled down the window and said angrily, "N****r, you don't deserve this, but maybe this will put some life in your pussy and make me some money! Two hours . . . two hours and I will be back, and you better have the extra money or your ass will be grass!"

Latrell held out his hand, palm down, and dropped a glassine baggy in Jewels's hand, which she quickly concealed as she walked away.

JEWELS ODOM COMMENTARY #1

The worst part of the game is getting squeezed by some loser john, white guys who come down from the Oakland hills looking for a little "nookie" that their white mamas couldn't give them. They all drive these very expensive cars looking to turn a fast trick for $100 bucks. Giving head is different; that goes for about $50 bucks, depending on my mood. After the johns, I have to deal with Latrell, my pimp, who will beat me if I am short the money.

When I first started working the streets, I only got burned a few times, but again, if I get squeezed, I have to find a way to make up the money, like lying and saying to Latrell that it's been slow or there is blue (cops) on the streets or maybe borrow money from one of the "Janes"—hookers—who are out doing the same, but everybody's time will come and the johns can only squeeze you once until the pimp finds out and deals with them big time.

One time some stupid white college kids came down to the hood after a UC frat party looking for some "nookie"—two football players thinking they're big men on campus, only this was ghetto time and place. After one lost a wallet, they went looking for the hooker who they said stole their wallet. It did not take long for their pimp to come in. He stabbed one kid in the chest and dropped him dead right there, and then stabbed the other kid, but that kid made it to the hospital and lived. We always tell those pretty white college boys to stay clear of us if they don't want some pimp coming after them because a pimp will kill you as sure as look at you.

In a dark, cold Oakland street alley, Jewels Odom sat at atop a trash can, lighting up a crack pipe. Tanya, a short, emaciated fourteen-year-old black girl, appeared out of the dark, her body language saying that she needed a hit from the pipe, but Jewels angrily pushed her away.

"Get the fuck away from me, n****r!" She pulled the pipe away and screamed, "I ain't in no fuckin' mood!"

Tanya moved closer to Jewels, her hands begging, until Jewels threw the pipe at her and walked away with a disgusted look on her face.

Jewels moved swiftly down the street, holding her boots in one hand, while stashing her drugs in her purse, which was stuffed with whatever she needed to get through the cold Oakland night. A blue BMW roadster pulled alongside her and honked loudly. Driving the BMW was a handsome, blond Caucasian male around 40 years old. The john stopped, climbed out of the BMW, and hurriedly fell into step with Jewels.

The john, hustling, asked, "How come you're not home doing your homework, honey?"

Jewels (styling) continued to walk. "This is my homework. I study losers like you all night."

"How much do you charge for some tutoring?"

"You're not in my league, flunky," she said, still styling. "I start at one hundred and work up."

The john lowered his voice and threw a suspicious look at Jewels. "I'm majoring in sociology. Can you help me pass my sociology exam?"

Finally, Jewels consented, "If you got the money, I got the exam, pencil dick!"

The john, still hustling and walking in stride, responded, "Look, I'll give you fifty bucks now and then another hundred later for your fine tutoring."

Jewels stopped and eyed him up and down.

"You ain't no scumbag, undercover asshole, are you?" she asked, examining his every move. She stuck out her nose like a dog and sniffed the john, saying, "Okay, loser, but you don't smell like anything I've been around."

The john took out a fifty-dollar bill from his wallet, but when Jewels reached for the bill, the john pulled out handcuffs from a back pocket and tried to snap them on Jewels's hand.

"Detention time!" he sneered.

"God daaaaaaaammmmmmm it! I knew you didn't smell like no john."

Jewels threw her boots at him, spun away, and took off running. The officer tried to chase after her until Jewels went into the afterburner speed and vanished into the night. Soon incoming sirens indicated that the police were giving chase. The winded officer picked up Jewels's spike-heeled boots, looked off in the distance, shook his head, and smiled. Frustrated, he threw both boots in Jewels's direction, and with a loud, condescending laugh, shouted, "You forgot something, Cinderella!"

Five minutes later, Jewels appeared in a dark, deserted Oakland alley, hunched over, coughing and spitting out mucus and blood. She could barely stand up and nearly fainted in exhaustion. She continued to cough and spit out blood. Out of nowhere, a pair of black shoes appeared. Then handcuffs were quickly snapped around Jewels's wrists.

"Well, if it isn't Jewels Odom," said the officer, "You got to give up those cigs. In the past, you could always outrun us, but look at you now girl. You can't run five blocks now without coughing your guts out. Well, in the hall you will have plenty of time to give up all those bad habits and clean yourself out. Ain't that right, Jewels?"

Jewels remained quiet, her body slumped in defeat.

JEWELS ODOM COMMENTARY #2

The Man on the Floor will take your dignity in body and mind. There is the pimp who will take your body first and then your mind by making you dependent on him in every respect.

There is the money issue, because if you are short, the pimp will beat you. There are the johns who try and squeeze you, which means you may be short on the money and then have to find a way to make up the difference for your pimp. In between are the street people who are always lurking, waiting for your pimp to throw you out so they can get a piece of you. There are the cops who will bust you, and finally there are the males at the hall who will simply get off on being the Man on the Floor.

TWO

Three Months Later

It was late afternoon. Brown leather shoes moved slowly down a long, dimly lit juvenile hall corridor. A few overhead lights cast a dark, intoxicating glow that cascaded off a polished green linoleum floor. The faint hum of the corridor's fluorescent lights and footsteps were the only sounds that could be heard in this aging 1950s correctional facility. The female residents had been locked in their cells like distant memories since 2:00 p.m., school dismissal time.

Louis Coles, a stocky black male about twenty-five years of age, appeared in black khaki pants and a black polo shirt with a golden juvenile corrections insignia patch on his jacket.

Louis yelled in a measured voice, "Man on the floor!"

A seductive female voice could be heard from behind a cell door: "This is Johnson. Is that you, Louis baby? I need to pee really, really bad!"

A second female's voice came from behind another cell, "I need my freakin' meds. You know I'm a manic depressant head case and you know I need my meds. I know you don't want me gettin' depressed, Louis, cuz, I just might decide to slit my wrists, and I know that would make you very, very unhappy Loooouis baby!"

A third female pleaded from another cell: "Louis, Tammy here. I need to freakin' pee really bad!"

Louis replied dryly, "Sorry, I didn't hear one please. Anyway, I'm not letting anyone out until shift change, and for those who have to pee, next time wear a goddamn diaper. No comment to the head case."

"Louis, why you so mean?" squealed a voice. "You know I can make you happy on the outs!"

"You keep talkin' and you'll be talkin' to yourself in your cell till Tito and night shift comes on and I don't need to tell you about Mr. Tito!"

Louis continued walking and finally stopped in front of cell door number 17 and yelled, "Pop seventeen! Pop seventeen!"

A loud buzzing sound came from the cold, gray metal door and then a click, and the metal door opened slightly. Louis peered into the dark cell as if he were rehearsing his next response and saw a curled-up blanketed body in a fetal position sleeping on the floor. A cement bed with a green plastic mattress, a wooden desk, a reading lamp, and a wooden chair were the only signs of furniture in the twelve-foot-by-twelve-foot cell surrounded by sterile white walls and two rows of florescent lights that lined the ceiling. A blanket covered a small window, preventing light from penetrating the small cell. Louis flipped on the light switch and violently pulled the blanket off the window.

"It's shooooooow time, Jewels. The party is over!" His voice was so loud, it echoed out to the hallway.

Jewels quickly covered her eyes with a blanket to shield herself from the piercing white light.

"Girl, did you hearrrrrrr me? I said, the party is over. It's show time and it's here comes da judge. He's waitin' with open arms and if he doesn't like what you're sellin,' it means I don't get to see your ugly face no more, cuz, you are goin' to the California Youth Authority or CYA, if you have trouble remembering."

Louis paused and waited impatiently for Jewels to climb out from under her blanket.

"And if da judge likes what you are sellin', it's still hasta la vista time and you go to that stupid emancipation something or other bullshit program and guess what—I win again!"

Jewels moved her tired body slowly until her head popped out of the blanket. She looked at Louis with tired eyes. Her skin was wrinkled from her nap and her bloodshot eyes were barely open. Regardless of her tired look, Jewels still presented an innate beauty. Her light-colored skin and long black hair with streaks of gold painted a picture of youthful beauty.

"I'm comin', n****r!"

Louis picked up a garbage bag filled with Jewels's clothes and then quickly dropped the bag on the floor.

He flashed a disgusted look and said angrily, "These clothes smell like shit. Cold turkey ain't easy. Ain't that right, Jewels? All that peein' and sweatin' . . . all that vomit. I'm going to downgrade you for not doing your laundry. That's assumin' you will be back. But I know that ain't goin' to happen, cuz it's the last of the ninth for bad ass Jewels Odom!"

Louis moved to the doorway and stood with his hands on his hips, a pissed-off expression on his face.

A female voice shouted from behind a cell door, "Louis, I really need to pee. Why you so mean?"

"I told you not until shift change. Now can it or I'll downgrade you!"

Louis continued to watch Jewels's tired body slowly get up.

She rubbed her bloodshot eyes and with attitude barked, "That's why they call it dirty laundry, asshole!"

Finally, Jewels followed Louis outside to the dark hallway. She was dressed in her usual juvie garb—orange jumpsuit, black Converse high-cut sneakers. She followed Louis down the long, dark hallway where Maria, a tall Hispanic woman, about thirty, worked at the front control desk. She spied Jewels and moved swiftly over to her, giving her a big hug, and whispered something in her ear. Jewels cracked a tense smile, nodded her head, and waited for Maria to flip a switch that unlocked a brown metal door leading to an outside corridor. The door opened with a click and Jewels followed Louis with arms folded tightly behind her back.

They moved through a series of dark hallways with empty cells, and then a few more metal white doors were opened by staff in different control rooms, and ultimately into the juvenile hall courtroom. An armed guard stood at the door. A black-haired woman in her late forties sat behind a long wooden table conferring with a female public defender, about thirty-five years of age.

Several adults sat in back on long brown wooden benches. The judge, a slight gray-haired man of about fifty years, dressed in a black robe, sat behind a large brown desk reading something from a folder. Jewels nervously stood in front of the judge, waiting for her sentence, while Louis sat in the corner with an angry smirk on his face. Jewels watched the judge's lips move rapidly but the only sound she could hear was a loud buzzing in her ears.

The judge adjusted his glasses and began to read loudly from a thick file, "January 20th, 2001 . . . soliciting sex from an undercover policeman.

March 3rd . . . selling a controlled substance to a minor. May 20th . . . committing a lewd act in public," and on and on.

The judge concluded reading Jewels's crimes and looked up, "This is your last chance. You have had three months at the hall to get your act together, Miss Odom, to stay out of the California Youth Authority. The Clark Academy, a residential school for juvenile offender girls, is willing to admit you in their Just Community or emancipation program." He shook his head, studied Jewels with piercing eyes, and looked down at Jewels's file. "Personally, there are probably many more deserving girls who would benefit from this program, because I am very concerned that you will not get through it. The only thing you have in your favor are your high test scores. If you hadn't scored so high on the IQ test, I would never have referred you." He repeated loudly, "NEVER! So, this is your call. If you bomb out of this program, I can guarantee that you will go to the California Youth Authority. Your age is now working against you. However, if you succeed at the Clark Academy—pass the GED, which I doubt—you'll be emancipated and your charges dropped."

Jewels continued to maintain a blank expression on her face.

The Judge addressed her again, but this time he was more emphatic: "Do . . . you . . . hear . . . me?!"

The judge's loud voice snapped Jewels out of her trance-like state. "Yes sir," she responded. "I think I can. Yes, I think I can."

"Think? Well, good luck, goodbye, and don't ever let me see you at the hall again."

JEWELS ODOM COMMENTARY #3

Understanding the different personalities of juvenile hall staff and volunteers can make your life a whole lot easier. Some staff (males) can be very kind and actually be supportive of the hole you got into. The kind and/or supportive males usually spent time at the hall as juvenile offenders, which might explain their support for us inmates. Those who never spent any time at the hall were the Louises of the world; either they hated the job or they were basically control freaks who got off on us girls. Juvenile hall line staff women can go in different directions as well. Some are motherly or sister-like, while others act like sergeants questioning your every move.

Volunteers are mostly kind and engaging and want to save the world. When you are released from the hall and then get busted and return, they will get really bent-out of shape and spend lots of time with you trying to understand why you couldn't get your shit together! Still, the best part about the hall are the volunteers like the guys who do great cooking classes because we never had such "grunts" on the streets. Also, there is a gardening program, which means we get to be outside and have fresh vegetables for dinner!

Another program is tai chi, which is taught by this really old dude who thinks he is the second coming of Jesus but he is always pissed off because most of the male inmates would rather talk to the girl inmates (the class was co-ed).

Another guy did moral development groups, which was very cool because you can challenge other staff when we did moral dilemmas like "would you steal a drug to save your dying wife," which 99 percent of male inmates would say, "No way, unless she cooked and cleaned for me and gave me good sex!"

Finally, there are the gang bangers which I never get involved with, but in the hall, when a new gang member shows up, it changes the energy, because staff are always on freaking out like a fight can break out at any time. If one gang member goes to the bathroom and has to pass a gang member from another gang, staff have to always be close by or between them to prevent them from flashing gang signs and then all hell can break loose. Anyway, that's life at the hall.

Jewels and Louis stood off to one side in the juvenile hall parking lot waiting for someone from the yellow Clark Academy school bus to appear. The parking lot was a nondescript area bordered by barbed-wire fences and a long, gray one-story building that housed about 150 inmates, age eleven to seventeen, about 30 percent white, 20 percent black, and 50 percent Hispanic.

JEWELS ODOM COMMENTARY #4

The history of juvenile hall inmates can be defined as extreme. My unit houses about thirty inmates, half of which are females and half males. The differences in age and offenses are probably the most interesting in extremes. For example, on my ward is a seventeen-year-old girl ex–gang banger who shot a girl in a gang fight. She is waiting for a hearing to find out if she is going to be sent to CYA (California Youth Authority). On the males' side is little Tommy, age 11, who ended up at the hall because his school principal found a Swiss Army knife in his backpack. His family had been backpacking the previous weekend and he forgot to take the knife out of his backpack. When a student told the teacher that little

Tommy had a knife in his backpack, one thing led to another and he was sus-
pended and sent to Juvie for bringing an assault weapon to school . . . hello?

One of the strangest incarcerations is fifteen-year-old Jason, who was sent to
the hall because during lunch he left his closed school campus for a coke. The boy
is a straight-A student, plays in the school band, and never had any problems
with the law. His problems began when a neighborhood friend asked him to come
down to see his new computer. The mother left the family car home. His friend
lived only about a mile away but Timmy decided to drive his mother's car to the
friend's house. The mother came home from lunch and found the car gone. She
called the police thinking the car was stolen. When Jason came home with the car
he discovered a police car in the driveway.

The mother didn't know what she should do since he didn't have a license and
he had never taken the car before. To teach him a lesson the policeman suggested
that Timmy be sent to juvenile hall for a twenty-four-hour hold. The mother
consented, but two weeks later at school lunchtime, Jason left his closed campus
for a coke. The school principal found out, called Timmy's PO, and because
Timmy now had a record, he was sent back to the hall for six months. As I said,
the hall has its extremes!

Jewels held a brown paper bag filled with her personal belongings close
to her body like a mother would hold a terrified child. Dr. Toni Barkley, a
tall, black-haired, white woman in her late thirties appeared from the
yellow school bus. Adolescent girls stuck their heads out of the bus's
windows like peeping toms and tried to get a better look at the new
student named Jewels Odom.

Chester sat in the driver's seat looking out from the open bus door
observing and rubbing his goatee. Chester, age forty-one, was the executive director of the Clark Academy. He was a light-skinned African
American man in his early forties and husband to Toni. He was dressed
casually with grey khaki pants, a blue shirt, and Nike running shoes. He
topped off his casual appearance with a green and gold yachting cap
with the letter *A* on it's front.

Louis walked slowly over to meet Toni and asked, "Are you Toni
Barkley from the Clark School."

"Yes, in flesh and blood honey!"

Louis, unimpressed by Toni's energy, passed a clipboard to Toni. "I'm
Louis Grimes. I need you to sign in three places and then loser girl is all
yours!"

Toni took the clipboard, hastily signed the form, and exclaimed, "And this wonderful girl must be Jewels!"

Jewels stood expressionless, alone and off to the side, continuing to hold her brown bag tightly against her body.

"Ha! What have you been smokin'?" Louis roared. "Jewels? Wonderful? I am so sick of her bad-ass personality and ugly face. Ohhhhh . . . meet miss mean. Ain't that right, loser girl?"

Toni ignored Louis and quickly handed the clipboard back to him with attitude.

"Don't ever let me see your ugly face here again, girl," he said, walking away, "cuz it will be here comes da judge and CYA—a nice name for prison!"

Toni extended her hand to Jewels but then laughed and said, "What am I doing? You need a big hug!" Toni moved quickly to Jewels and gave her a big hug.

"Honey, now you're all mine! That's right sweetie, you don't have to deal with the man on da floor no more. Let's get on the bus and we'll take you to your new home."

Jewels looked over at the Clark School girls staring out of the bus's window with a defensive expression.

"Oh yes," Toni said, putting her arm around Jewels. "I forgot to mention, whenever we get a new student, we like to bring some of the girls as a welcoming committee. Today we only brought eight of the thirteen Clark Academy girls. The other five are presently at school on restriction."

"Please follow me," said Toni, moving toward the bus.

Jewels slowly followed Toni to the beat-up yellow school bus.

When Jewels boarded the bus, Chester stuck out his hand and prevented Jewels from passing.

Jewels flashed him a disgusted look.

Chester continued to hold out his hand to prevent Jewels from passing.

"Girl, that'll be a fiver pleeeeeease! Don't you know that nothing is free in life?"

Jewels gave Toni a confused look.

"Excuse me, Jewels, but the jokester bus driver is Chester, my husband and so-called executive-director-slash-comedian. He talks a good game, but if anyone on the streets should ever bother you, Chester will take care of you. Ain't that right, honey?"

"Oh yea," responded Chester. "I can call 911 with the best of them. Now, Jewels come on now. I had you thinking, didn't I? I was only playin' with you, girl, but you really were going to give me a fiver?"

"He's got a weird sense of humor but I still love him. He's my hubby. I guess I have to till death do us part. Ain't that right, honey?"

"Oh yea, but you need to talk to my agent first," he said, winking at Toni.

Jewels shook her head in disgust, then turned in a huff and walked straight down to an empty seat. She sat down and looked straight ahead, ignoring the girls who just snickered and laughed.

DJ, a very large, rotund African American girl, sang out like some jazz singer, "Ohhhhhh don't listen to the old dude. He thinks he's Fred Sanford or something!"

DJ punctuated her response with a loud fart, causing all the girls to scream and stick their heads out of the bus's windows to breathe.

Chester grabbed his chest like he'd been shot. "I heard that! Real cold, DJ. Real cold!"

Toni stood up at the front of the bus and said, "Now that DJ has exhibited her true intelligence, can everyone please get back in your seats" Ladies, this is Jewels Odom, our newest student to the Clark Academy."

The girls turned to Jewels, made brief eye contact, and then turned back to Toni, who said, "Now, can we please get this show on the road and get our bodies and lives back to where we really belong?"

The negative energy that permeated the bus between Jewels and the girls was extreme. The handwriting on the wall was always this way when a new student would begin at the school. That is, who was going to be "shop bully" or "top dog" always took center stage, and the new student—like any new "top dog" to the pack or group—would have to prove herself over and over again that she was not going to take any shit from anyone. They had all come from the streets and they were professionals in the game of survival and street smarts. The difference between Jewels and the girls was her look, which was what they described in their minds right away as a "zebra," or half white and half black. Jewels always assumed that her daddy was white and her mother was black. Also, Jewels was very tall, about 5 feet 10 inches, which gave her a certain stature among the girls and one that on the streets the johns always admired. Combine all these attributes together along with her street smarts, and you had all the making of a "shop bully," which was why the tension was so high on the bus.

Chester pulled down his gold and green Oakland A's yachting cap, released the emergency break, and with a jolt from the engine, the bus roared loudly away, leaving the juvenile hall parking lot and its barbed-wire fences alone in the cold, foggy distance.

Chester turned his cap around and reached for the bus's intercom, which dangled from the ceiling like an old ornament that had seen better days.

When Chester attempted to speak into the microphone, it let out a loud piercing screech that blasted throughout the old bus.

"Sorrrrrry! Let me try again," he said over the microphone. "Goooooood afternooooon laaaaadies! This is Chester your friendly school bus driver, executive director, tour guide, and bill-payer. Welcome aboard the Clark Academy Express. Our cruising speed will be about forty miles per hour, depending on the traffic and wind gusts. Arrival time should be about thirty-two minutes."

"Can we pleeeeeeease go on quiet or stupid mode?" yelled DJ from the back of the bus. Chester ignored DJ and continued his imitation of a friendly tour guide.

"Again, depending on traffic and attitude, or do I mean altitude?" Chester looked in the rearview mirror for a response, but the girls remained silent, looking bored.

Again, DJ responded with a loud "Pleeeeeeeeeease Fred, no more. You're killin' me!"

Chester stopped his tour guide imitation and turned on the radio to Tracy Chapmen's song "Over the Line" and quickly the girls became energized and began to sing along.

Chester turned the bill of his cap to the front when the song ended and returned to the microphone.

"Ladies, Chester here again! Now, I want to remind you about all the popular places that you girls could be visiting someday — that is, if you don't figure this game out."

Denise, the only white girl in the program, began to sing the song "The Game of Love." She sang the first line, "The game of love baby," and then the girls chimed in, "Love, in love, in love baaaaaaby!"

Chester waited for the girls to finish singing and continued to speak over the microphone. "Now over there just to the right is San Quentin, home to such notable creeps as Charles Manson, Sirhan Sirhan. You remember Charlie and his gang of creeps!" Chester pointed his finger in another direction: "And way over there is Alcatraz, but the good news is you won't be going there because it closed years ago, but it still should serve as a reminder to the be-good-or-be-gone crowd. Someday a good field trip, but only as tourists."

Most of the girls maintained tired, bored looks until DJ, who was lying down in her seat, began to mimic Chester: "And over there are a bunch of seagulls pooping all over the cars."

Chester turned to Toni and asked, "Do you want me to go into the history of the Manson Gang?"

Toni shook her head in frustration: "No and please just watch the road, Mr. Comedian."

Chester put away the microphone and proceeded to get into serious driving mode. The bus pulled off the highway and onto the Oakland streets. The girls gawked at the street people like they all knew them. There were panhandlers doing their thing, several old males brown-bagging or drinking, and a few homeless individuals with signs that said, "Jesus saves if you share some $!"

When Chester down-geared, the bus gave a jerk, which made the girls snicker at Chester, like he was some old dude who didn't know how to drive.

Chester responded to the girls' snickers and catcalls by turning on the microphone and making an even louder "blaaaaaaaas," which only made the girls unleash more catcalls and snickers, until Toni jumped in. "This ain't ding dong school, so can we be a little more mature? And that goes for everyone, including you, Mr. Ding Dong Executive Director!"

Chester looked over at Toni with an incredulous look and began singing, "Why is everybody always picking on me?"

JEWELS ODOM COMMENTARY #5

We pull next to a school bus with a group of public-school kids . . . nine- and ten-year-olds going somewhere. I spot one black girl sitting alone on the bus and she reminds me of myself when I was about the same age. We make eye contact and her eyes seem to ask, Why is someone so old doing on a broken-down school bus?

The young girl brings me back to when I was about her age and living in a residential school for sexually abused kids ages six to twelve. These were very crazy kids who had been taken from their homes because they had been sexually molested. I was sent from a foster home to this school because two twelve-year-old boys tried to rape me. The different stories as to why we were sent to this program would make you sick! Kids as young as five would stay in this program for about six months, and then get sent back home and within a month they were back at our school because they were molested again. They called it reunification or when kids get reunified with their bio-parents. It was insane and repeated over and over again!

"Good afternoon, ladies," shouted Chester over the microphone. "I am back. I mean I'm really back—your wonderful, handsome, smart tour guide again!"

Chester looked over at Toni and asked, "Did I forget anything sweetheart?"

Toni lifted one eyebrow but remained quiet.

"I'm about to give you a bird's-eye view of the local Oakland scum and what some of you can look forward to if you decide to run or refuse to follow your program. On your right side is old Rosie, who never turned down a trick in her life. She's only thirty-five, but as you can see, she looks about seventy. Sadly, she could have any of the diseases that you catch when you're sellin' your bodies on the street like clap, syphilis, gonorrhea, herpes I and II, and the granddaddy of them all: HIV. These are some of the perks when you whore but I don't have to remind you about that, right?"

Chester looked in the rearview mirror to see if he got a rise from the girls but the girls only squirmed in their seats with deadpan looks.

"And on your right, over there in front of the liquor store, is Willie the local drunk and wannabe pimp. He has been out of prison now for the past month, but he'll take your money and even your life at the drop of a dime. When it comes to slime, this guy's a perfect ten plus. Oh, but I don't have to tell you girls about the Willies of the world. Some of you have had associations with the Willies of the world and tragically some of you may even have had their babies! Sad, really sad!"

The Clark Academy bus rumbled up through the Oakland hills, passing well-kept, new three-story homes with immaculate yards. They reached Clark Street and pulled in front of a graying three-story mansion. Some of the mansion's siding was falling off and the lawn had seen better days. The large three-story building sat among newer homes like an old battleship that had been put in mothballs. Fortunately, Chester and Toni had procured grant money, and with the help of some very liberal neighbors, they got permission for the old mansion to be turned into a school for juvenile offenders.

Standing in a driveway across the street from the school was neighbor Mrs. Jackson, a gray-haired black woman in her seventies. When she heard the loud Clark Academy bus roaring up the street, she grabbed her old dog Louis and ran frantically to the front door of her one-story home like she was escaping a swarm of bees. Once she was at the door, she stopped and watched what else might unfold from those "bad Clark Academy girls."

The Clark Academy bus grinded to a noisy, smoky stop at the curb. The school bus door hissed open like a teapot ready to explode and then a thud. First, Toni stepped off the bus, followed by the Clark School students, who pushed and shoved their way out the door.

Mrs. Jackson flashed a scowling look at the bus and said to Louis, "Oh my God! Those bad girls and their crazy director and wife are back turning our quiet neighborhood into a ghetto. Why they ever allowed this school to be put here I will never know!"

As soon as the girls saw their three-story academy/home, they raced up the driveway, climbed the five steps, and barreled through the front screen door. DJ was the slowest and one of the last students to the front door. However, the screen door slammed shut just as DJ reached the screen door, and she crashed through the door, knocking herself and the door to the floor.

Jewels was the last to disembark from the bus and walked slowly into the school building almost like a scared, trapped animal. She didn't go directly upstairs to her bedroom. Instead she began to explore the downstairs of the old mansion. She walked through a large room filled with beat-up tables, couches, chairs, and rugs, accentuated by high cathedral ceilings and a large fireplace that was literally filled with trash. She proceeded into another hallway and then up the back stairs until she found a bathroom. She attempted to close the door but instead became fascinated by the doorknob and began to obsess on it. She turned the doorknob one way, then another, until her hand felt like it was stuck to the doorknob.

The experience of actually being able to open a real door and not having to wait for juvenile hall control to open the metal cell door gave her a liberating feeling. Next, Jewels looked in the medicine cabinet and found a box of sanitary napkins and screamed, "Go to hell, Man on the Floor!"

The anger in her body gave her a brief reprieve that she would not have to ask the Man on the Floor for a tampon. Next, she turned to the toilet and flushed that several times. Lastly, she turned on the sink's faucet and compulsively washed her hands over and over again.

Toni appeared on the second floor, anxiously walking back and forth, making sure the girls were all in their bedrooms. Soon, she realized that Jewels was missing from her bedroom and hurriedly rushed back to the top of the stairway.

"Jewels Odom!" she yelled, her voice booming throughout the large old mansion,

"Where are you, girl? You are not allowed to roam, unless I tell you to roam!"

Jewels raced out of the bathroom like she was escaping a bad dream and nearly knocked Toni over.

"Whoa, slow down, girl! You'll have a whole year to roam in this old lady home. For now, however, you need to hang out in your bedroom, which is number 4. Down the hall. You'll room with darling Angel."

Jewels had a fearful look on her face that she would be downgraded or sent back to juvie, but this was not case. Instead, Toni said in a kind voice, "Okay, I know what you are going through. You are like a child who has not had candy in a while and now you're in a candy store. Just relax and leave the driving to us. *Tú entiendes?*"

JEWELS ODOM COMMENTARY #6

When you get out of the hall and are living in a real home, you notice all these weird behaviors that you begin to do because of all the time you spent cooped up in a jail cell. Suddenly, you have some freedom like turning on and off running water (in the hall the water flow was timed), doorknobs instead of being locked up, and having to yell, "Pop three!" to be let out, and line staff saying you got only one minute to pee or to take a dump. Why do I need to wash my hands over and over again? Maybe I am trying to wash the memory of being a hoe off my body.

THREE

A New Teacher Principal Man

Anthony Romero, age thirty-five, parked his 1970 gray Saab station wagon in front of the three-story stucco-colored mansion-turned–Clark Academy, about thirty yards behind a parked police car. He climbed out of his car, surveying the neighborhood as if he were a real estate broker looking to sell a home. He scanned a slip of paper to ensure that he had the correct street and house number. He nodded his head and wondered how this school for ex-juvenile-offender girls was ever allowed in this charming upscale neighborhood. He climbed back into his car and waited nervously for his 3 p.m. interview for the Clark Academy teacher/principal position.

His ivy league appearance was wrapped in a brown corduroy jacket, black dress pants, blue shirt, and black tie, his thick black hair was combed back, parted in the middle, and he sported a trim black beard. If you didn't know any better, you would assume he had the look of a lost college professor. Being a recent graduate from the same Harvard program that the two executive directors Toni and Chester Barkley had attended was a major reason, he suspected, for him being considered for the job as teacher/director.

In the cult of Just Communities, he thought he possessed knowledge that other candidates for the job did not have, a reality that could soon be short-lived when dealing with the Clark Academy staff and students.

The job description specified that candidates have experience working with inner-city at-risk girls, ages seventeen to twenty-one. Anthony had only worked with at-risk and mostly white kids, ages sixteen to twenty-one, in a rural Connecticut day treatment school. However, the Clark Academy girls were major league when it came to the less pejorative term *at risk*, since they all had spent time in juvenile hall and/or residential treatment programs, and another more pejorative term *S.E.D.* (seriously emotional disturbed). Also, the Clark Academy girls were intercity and multiracial with a proximity to the hardcore streets of Oakland and San Francisco.

Their geographic location to the inner city was a major cause of why these girls were hardcore when it came to crime that included prostitution, drug dealing, gang banging, and so on. In short, Anthony's previous experience and cliental were minor league, including breaking and entering, car theft, assault and battery toward teachers, and so on. Again, it was Anthony's knowledge of the Just Community and his studies with his advisor at Harvard that could give him an edge over other applicants as Clark Academy principal.

Finally, the position could be dangerous as he tried to navigate his students through their day-to-day educational programs, while supporting enrichment programs in art, music, and vocational education opportunities encumbered by the dangerous San Francisco and Oakland street people lying in wait to steal the girls back to their negative pasts.

Anthony waited impatiently in his car while staring at a police officer who was speaking with a Hispanic youth on the sidewalk in front of the school.

Mrs. Jackson mumbled to herself as she and her tired old dog, Louis, passed by Anthony's car on their everyday walk.

"I've lived in this neighborhood for thirty-plus years and things were going along just fine. For heaven's sake, now we are not even safe up here in the hills. Soon, there will be drug dealers and prostitutes, all because they allowed this school and these bad girls into our neighborhood!"

Anthony flashed a puzzled look at her and remained quiet.

Executive director Dr. Toni Barkley, dressed in a neat black pantsuit, appeared in the school's front door and casually walked to where the officer and the Hispanic youth were standing and addressed the officer in a friendly tone: "Good afternoon officer. Is there a problem?"

The officer answered in an official voice: "A neighbor called and said there was a strange vehicle in the neighborhood. When I got here I found two teenage boys hanging out in their car. One said he's a friend of a girl named Angel who lives or goes to school here. He wants to drop off this bag of clothes. I offered to deliver the clothes myself, and after some resistance from one of the boys who wanted to personally give the clothes to the girl himself, he agreed and asked if I could give the clothes to her. They left and there wasn't any problem."

Toni smiled and explained, "Oh yes, homeboys. We are a group home for juvenile offenders. Some of or our girls' so-called homeboys are probably making a move, just letting our girls know they are around. Gang affiliation is always a hassle for our girls who are trying to get away from their homeboys. Our girls know the rules: any fraternizing with their homeboys means immediate expulsion and back to the hall or even CYA. Mrs. Jackson, our neighbor across the street, always freaks out when she sees strangers in the hood, especially young males. She is old and not used to having the likes of our girls nearby, nor their homeboys, if you get my drift. She fought tooth and nail against getting a group home in this neighborhood, but thank God for some kind neighbors up here in the hills and a grant from the state, which provided the money to buy this old mansion; bottom line—who knows where our girls would be?"

The officer listened carefully, taking mental notes about the school, girls, and Mrs. Jackson.

"For these girls," continued Toni, "this is truly their last chance to break out of a system of crime. We are an emancipation program, which means they can get their GED's, graduate, and leave their tragic past sins behind. Halleluiah! Although, some may be whistling in the wind, others could graduate with a high school diploma. I expect you will get more calls from Mrs. Jackson. Anyhow, thanks for coming to her or our rescue."

The officer nodded his head and passed the bag of clothes to Toni. They talked for a few more minutes, and then the officer returned to his car and drove off.

Anthony Romero continued to sit in his car, nervously checking his watch.

Toni looked over at Mrs. Jackson's home, shook her head, and cast a friendly wave in her direction, as the older woman continued to spy on Toni from her front door. Toni turned and walked up to the school's front porch, where Kim, a light-skinned girl, age eighteen, and Jasmine, a tall, stocky nineteen-year-old black girl, were listening to rap music and smoking cigarettes, parading around in their pink bathrobes and purple slippers.

Toni stopped a few feet from the two girls: "And you two airheads . . . keep the rap down. This ain't East Oakland, you know, and do not let me see one cigarette butt on the ground or it will be your butts on restriction!" She turned and walked to the front door, stopped and without turning to face the girls said, "and why are you both in your bathrobes and slippers at this time of the day? This ain't some massage parlor! Go upstairs and get dressed before I pull you both up!"

Anthony continued to sit in his car, nervously checking his watch, looking out at the school, then back to his watch. He looked at himself in the rearview mirror, then again back to his watch.

Kim spied Anthony in the car and yelled, "Hey mister, are you the new teacher director man, or just some freaked-out peeping Tom!"

The two girls giggled and began to seductively dance and gyrate to the loud rap music that was reverberating throughout the neighborhood.

Anthony ignored their response and again looked nervously at his watch, which said *3 p.m.,* the time of his interview.

Finally, he climbed out of his car and walked slowly to the porch where Kim and Jasmine were still dancing to the loud rap music.

"This *is* the Clark Academy?" he asked tentatively.

The rap music blasted so loudly that the girls only shook their heads and motioned with their hands that Anthony was only an annoyance to them.

Again, Anthony shouted, "*Is* this the Clark Academy?"

The two girls shot more annoying looks at him. Finally, he climbed the five steps leading up to the front porch, walked over to the CD player, and proceeded to turn the rap music down.

He lowered his voice and again asked, "Is this the Clark Academy? Is this the Clark school?"

Both girls glared at Anthony, shocked that he not only just lowered their music but also that he touched their boom box.

"Who are you?!" yelled Kim. "And why did you put you put your white honkie fingers on my CD player? And by the way . . . I ain't hard of hearin'. . . . Maybe this is the Clark Academy and maybe it ain't. So, what will you give me if I said yes . . . whatever you name is, Mr. white honkie man with no name!"

Anthony composed himself and said directly, "My name is Anthony Romero and I have an appointment with Dr. Chester Barkley."

Kim looked at Anthony straight in the eye, shook her head, and replied, "You talkin' about Fred . . . like in Fred Sanford, the famous junk dealer?"

Anthony looked down at a slip of paper and stuttered, "Ahhhhh, no, no, I mean Dr. Barkley. I have a 3 p.m. appointment. This is the Clark Academy?"

"Man, are you sure you got the right place?" questioned Kim in a softer, less antagonistic voice. "We thought you were here to buy furniture. . . . You see, Fred or Chester is into buying junk furniture, but he thinks they are like antiques, like he thinks he will make millions someday. We think this school is only a front for his stupid furniture racket!"

"But is this a school or an academy?" asked Anthony staring intensely at the girls in pink bathrobes and purple slippers at 3 p.m. in the afternoon.

"Yea," said Jasmine, shaking her head and body. "Well, Mr. No Name, it's like *this*. Our sub-teacher is sick and well, we got sick of her too!"

"Yea, that's right," interrupted Kim, "we got another day off, because our sub-teacher was sick, like crazy sick!" Then Kim turned to Jasmine, gave her a high five, laughed, and spun around like a top, and then both girls said in unison, "like sick of us!"

"That's not funny," voiced Jasmine in a sympathetic tone, "but you know she has been sick a lot these days."

Again, Kim high-fived Jasmine and said, "Like you got that right," and they screamed again, "like she is sick, sick of us!"

They both exchanged high fives again and started laughing and dancing around in circles. Finally, Kim motioned with her hands for Anthony to go into the school.

Kim moved back to her boom box, turned up the rap music, and the two girls started dancing again, but not without sensuously shaking their bodies and waving goodbye to Anthony. Anthony, not to be outdone, shook his body to the music, nodded his head, and said, "Mr. No Name is Mr. Anthony Romero, so don't get too happy ladies, because I'll be back!"

Next, Anthony slid through the front door into a dark hallway as rap music played, and three girls argued over who was going to get to use the pay phone. Cautiously, he stepped over another girl curled up on the floor in a blanket and stood motionless in the hallway until Angel, a short, thin Hispanic girl around seventeen, walked over to him and pulled him out of the haze and noise.

She moved closer to Anthony. "You got a cigarette?"

Anthony, startled, pulled back, "Errrrr, sorry, I don't smoke."

"Well, that's a sorry-ass answer if I ever heard!" Then Angel swaggered away to a nearby couch and proceeded to curl up in a blanket.

Anthony turned his attention to a pay phone where three girls were still battling for possession.

"I don't care who your mama is!" screamed one girl. "If you don't get off the damn phone, I goin' to pull you and your big fat mama off in a second!"

A short, rotund black woman around fifty appeared from another room. Her voice boomed out, "If I hear any more noise from any of you, you will find yourself on Front Street!"

She looked over at Angel curled up on the couch and shouted, "Girl, you need to go upstairs and clean you room. This ain't no flop house!"

Next, she returned to the three girls battling over the pay phone. "You know Mrs. T. don't play and tells no lies. That pay phone will be gone if you don't stop with all the wolfing!"

Anthony stayed rooted in the dark corner of the hallway, taking in all the drama until Mrs. T. spied Anthony standing alone in the corner.

Mrs. T. let out a loud laugh, shook her head and said, "Now child, I see you over there all alone. You can't hide from old Mrs. T. I mean nobody and I mean nobody hides from Thelma M. Thompson. You know I have eyes in the back of my head and you can take that to the bank or to President Bush or whoever!"

Next, she explained, "You must be here for the director-teacher interview? Well, whatever you are here for, you better come with me, cuz these girls will eat you up, child, and spit you out before you can blink an eyelash. They are rude to the core and know the walk and the talk, so you better watch your step." Then she whispered, "Men are a rare species in this school. Now you follow me child. Mr. Chester or whoever is waitin' for you."

She made a quick turn to the rest of the girls: "I will be right back and any more noise about that damn pay phone and you'll all end up on Front Street!" She shook her body to the words "Front Street" and continued, "You know Mrs. T. don't play. Mrs. T. tells no lies and you know where you can take that."

When Mrs. T. turned her back, several girls made faces and imitated her by shaking their bodies. Mrs. T. stopped on the stairwell and said, "You know Mrs. T. has eyes in the back of her head, so if you're doin' what I think you're doin', I will deal with you all later." She lowered her voice, "Now, I have to take care of this gentleman who must be out of his mind to want to work with you rude, nasty children!"

Anthony followed Mrs. T. up a dark stairway, stepping over a few more girls who were in blankets, curled up in fetal positions.

Mrs. T. announced loudly, "Man on the floor! Man on the floor!"

She stopped and turned to Anthony and said in a serious voice, "Whenever a man, any man, is upstairs, you got to yell 'man on floor,' because you do not want to get caught in any compromising situations, especially with this crew. Mrs. T. tells no lies!"

Anthony and Mrs. T. made a couple of quick turns, then down a long, narrow hallway to a door labeled "Front Street—Your Last Hope"—Dr. Chester Barkley, Executive Director—Clinical Director: Dr. Toni Barkley.

A few girls were standing out in front of the door with impatient expressions.

When a short black girl named Patricia spied Anthony and Mrs. T, she confronted them: "I get to see Chester first because I have been waitin' here the longest and I need freakin' laundry money because I think I'm beginning to smell like Chester!"

Bonita, a stocky black girl, interrupted Patricia: "Ahhhhhhh no, I need to speak to him about goin' home this weekend. It's my grannie's birthday!"

Mrs. T. ignored both girls and knocked gently on Chester's door.

Chester's voice thundered out from behind the closed door: "If you are seventeen years or older, I do not wish to be disturbed, even if it's your birthday or you have won the lottery, or maybe you want to donate to my upcoming birthday fund—the same goes for all you!"

Mrs. T. hesitated for a moment and then responded, "Mr. Chester, it's me, Thelma."

She turned to Anthony and said with a wink, "Sorry, your name again?"

"Romero . . . Anthony Romero."

"Mr. Romeo is here for his interview for the teacher/director position."

Anthony flashed an embarrassed look and repeated, "No, it's Romero . . . Romero."

Chester yelled back impatiently, "Whatever! Just send the poor man in! Send in Romeo and if you like you can even send in Juliet as well. Just send them both in. I can't handle all these interruptions. How's a man ever goin' to get anything done in this asylum?"

When Mrs. T. opened the door, the girls all rushed the door, demanding to see Chester.

"I need to go to my grannie's birthday!"

"I want a new social worker!"

"I need more laundry money!"

"I need counseling with Toni!"

"Tell Mrs. T. to stop picking on me!"

While Mrs. T. guarded the opening to the door, Anthony slid quickly through and into a very small, cluttered office.

"I told you I can't talk to any of you now. Maybe later, or after I had my evening cocktail and a backrub from Toni. Mrs. T, please control the natives . . . inmates, whatever!"

"In your dreams," responded Toni with a laugh. "In your dreams, my darling."

Mrs. T. closed the half-opened door, while a few girls tried to stick their heads into the opening at the same time and continued their demands: "I need laundry money. I need a weekend pass!"

Chester was dressed in a light-blue three-piece suit, white shirt, without a tie. He sat behind a cluttered desk of papers and books. Next to him sat Toni, who was dressed in a sharp, dark, black pantsuit. A beat-up old lamp sat atop Chester's desk with no lamp shade; piles of clothes lay in every corner, and the one bookcase that surrounded the room was stuffed haphazardly with books. A torn couch sat in front of Chester's untidy desk. The dark, disorderly room had no windows, which only accentuated the room's chaotic appearance.

Chester responded to Anthony's arrival with a terse, "Thank you, Thelma, and can you please tell the natives to keep it down or I'm going to pull that damn pay phone out and they can start communicating by mail or even Morse code if need be!"

Mrs. T. responded from behind the closed door with a firm, "Yes sir! I told them they would be heading to Front Street if they didn't get their act together!"

Chester rose from his chair and introduced himself: "I'm Chester Barkley and this is my significant other or wife, Toni, our clinical director."

Toni blew Chester a kiss and repeated, "Significant other . . . you're a romantic at heart!"

Chester smiled and tapped his heart.

First, Anthony shook Toni's hand, then Chester's, and sat down on the beat-up couch. When Anthony sat down on the couch, it seemed to suck him further down, so that when Chester and Toni sat down, they were about a foot taller than Anthony, which made the couch sitter feel dwarfed. Anthony tried to adjust his position to look or feel taller, but it was useless, so he just sat back down and remained quiet, waiting for Chester's next act to begin. From Anthony's perspective, Chester seemed to fit his role perfectly. His look and speech actually reminded Anthony of Red Fox, who played the part in the TV show *Sanford and Son*. He was light-skinned with a goatee.

Most of all, he had a sense of confidence that surrounded his every move and word. His speech was filled with numerous one-liners that were often comical, yet street-wise with a certain intelligence. Again, his personality seemed perfectly suited for the population he was working with. The constant bantering with the girls was like a continuous surrealistic play or stand-up comedy routine that never seemed to end. And then there was Toni, who fit his energy perfectly. She was smart, confident, and educated, which balanced out the interracial marriage perfectly. Finally, let's not forget they both had PhD's from Harvard, which only added spice to the surrealistic running play.

Chester sat back in his chair as if he were ready to go for a leisurely drive. "Please don't pay too much attention to the crazies; things usually run smoothly. Isn't that right dear?"

Toni rolled her eyes and laughed. "Don't bullshit the man. The place is like a psycho ward! The girls are going bonkers because you are too cheap to hire a real teacher/principal man or woman or whatever. Mr. Tightwad thinks he can get by with substitute teachers. Hello!"

"Please excuse my impudent wife, but she gets this emotional illness . . . it's called speaking her mind."

A loud banging suddenly came from Chester's office door. The force was so great that the banging nearly knocked some books off a nearby bookcase.

"What, is this Avon calling?" he yelled. "Well, I ain't buying or sellin', so, go away, cuz your banging is goin' to give us all an Excedrin headache."

A girl's voice began to yell loudly from behind the office door. "It's me, Patricia, and I ain't buyin' or sellin' nuthin' You promised me more laundry money and I'm here to get it. I know my rights! You know my mama didn't raise no fool!"

"Hey! No Fair," returned Chester, winking at Anthony. "Hey, No Fair . . . you can't bring your mama in. Anyway, did you forget you have *no* rights here and you can tell your mama I said that!"

When Chester spoke, his eyes got wide and his body moved as he enunciated each word.

"Anyways, you couldn't pass a pee test today if you tried and you can take that to your PO, social worker, mama, or whoever."

He turned to Anthony and held up his hand as though to say, *Watch this. She is going to lose her mind.* Then he shouted, "And don't forget, I saved you from the pimps and pushers in Oakland and there was juvie and here comes da judge, and remember what Toni said? I needed to see a shrink for giving you this last chance. So pleeeeeeeease don't bang on my door, cuz it could give me Excedrin headache number 2, so no more wolfing!"

Patricia responded in a controlled but angry voice. "My social worker told me I should be gettin' five dollars more a week for laundry. My mama didn't raise no fool!"

"Maybe you should get the money from your social worker," he shouted, "since she got all the answers and the taxpayer's money!"

While all this was going on, Anthony just sat quietly on the couch with this incredulous expression that said, *I have only been at the school or no more than thirty minutes and already I'm emotionally drained. It started with the two girls dancing on the porch in bathrobes, girls lying on the floor curled up in blankets like dead bodies, and now Chester and Toni's act!*

Finally, Chester motioned for Toni to open the door; she looked at him with the expression like, *Do you really want to go there?*

Chester looked at Toni with wide eyes and a nod of the head.

When Toni opened the door, she rushed quickly back to her chair.

Standing in the doorway was Patricia, a short, black girl about seventeen, but who looked about ten and weighed no more than 110 pounds. She remained rooted in the in the doorway, eyes casting daggers in every direction.

Toni pretended to cower in her chair and said, "Pleeeeeeeease, don't you try and hurt me now girl!"

Patricia remained silent and continued to shoot more daggers at Chester.

Chester turned his attention to Anthony. "Mr. Romeo, this is Patricia. Now, you wouldn't think that a sweet little thing like Patricia could wolf like that."

Anthony returned, "It's Romero. not Romeo."

"Sorry, Mr. Romerrrrrrrrrro!"

Patricia made no effort to make eye contact with Anthony. Instead, her brown, piercing eyes remained riveted on Chester.

Next, Chester asked calmly, "Now, why all the noise? You don't have to bang on my door like some crazy. And girlie girl," he continued, "you think we were born yesterday. You want more money to buy weed. I been around that block before. Your pee test is coming up, and if you flunk, you is goin', goin', gone back to juvie and you don't even have to tell that to da judge!"

"That's not true. I need laundry money!"

Toni remained quiet and then uttered, "Maybe we can compromise. How about four dollars a week more?"

Chester nearly fell out of his chair: "What! Maybe you need to take a pee test? If I give this girl four dollar a week extra, then I will have to give the rest of the natives four dollars a week. Have you lost your mind? I mean you do have a PhD from Harvard, or maybe it was a mail-order degree and as sure as my name is Chester P. Barkley I hope it don't mean post-hole-digger either!"

Chester placed his face in his hands and said with a laugh, "You know you are goin' to create anarchy here."

Toni responded, "Just a thought, dear."

"No way am I going to be shaken down for that kind of money. No way, Jose!"

"I knew it!" Patricia cried. "You want the money only for yourself, so you can go on a vacation with old dudes like Bob Hope or stupid old people like that!"

"Oh, yeah," Chester, said examining his hand. "Like Palm Springs. Yeah, like I need to work on my tan?"

He turned to Anthony and asked pointedly, "Mr. Romero, does this look like I need a tan? Toni needs one for her lilywhite skin, but as you can see, not me. My tan goes back thousands of years. Maybe the two of you can go to Palm Springs and party with Bob Hope, except I think he is dead."

"No dear, I think he's still alive. Am I right Mr. Romero?"

Anthony just shook his head, unsure.

Chester looked over at Anthony with a concerned look. "I hope Patricia is not scaring you."

"No, I'm good . . . really," Anthony said, adjusting his posture for the hundredth time.

"I'm goin' to call my social worker," threatened Patricia, "and she's goin' to close this pimp school down!"

Finally, a frustrated Patricia burst out the door to a chorus of voices that appeared from outside the office.

"I need a weekend pass!"

"I need more money for my hair!"

"I need my money for my weekend furlough!"

"I'm hungry. What's for dinner?"

"I need to see my grannie!"

Toni quickly closed the door and began to scan Anthony's resume.

"Okay, enough of this nonsense. Mr. Romero, how would you solve our dilemma with Patricia?"

Anthony didn't hesitate: "I would probably go with her to the laundromat to see if she really does need the money."

Toni nearly fell from her chair and screamed, "That's the best damn answer I have heard this entire week! Maybe the month. Hire this man!"

"Not a bad answer," Chester remarked calmly. "So, you got Toni auditioning for some soap opera or the *Gong Show*, and you got some experience, but mostly with JFK's kids, and you got all these gaps in employment, like every year you take time off to hang out on some Santa Barbara beach or play golf with John Travolta. However, I will overlook all that, but what we need is a reality show to see if you can really teach our wonderful, civilized ladies. Also, I will call Larry as in Kohlberg from Harvard to check you out as well. I mean you did go there, right?"

Anthony nodded his head.

"Okay," he continued. "Let's see if you can do a demo lesson this evening with our ladies . . . about 6:30 p.m.? In short, we would like to see if you can demonstrate a facsimile of a class and I don't mean breakfast, lunch, and dinner. Bottom line! Get them to pass the GED by June without you or any one of them getting killed. You do have an insurance policy? Just joking."

Anthony thought for a moment and slowly got up out of his seat, extended his hand to Toni and then to Chester, and said, "Okay, tonight at six-thirty. You're on. What I'll teach, I do not know."

"With this crowd, there will be times when you will have to be spontaneous or fly by the seat of your pants," declared Toni. "That is the truth if you expect to succeed at this job, so this should be a good challenge for you."

Anthony shook Toni's hand and then Chester's hand and said, "Let the games begin at 6:30 p.m."

JEWELS ODOM COMMENTARY #7

There was all this craziness about this new Harvard dude being hired as our teacher. DJ was taking bets that tightwad Chester would never spend the money to hire the poor guy. Personally, I give DJ five-to-one odds it will never happen. Well, as you know we have been going through sub-teachers like DJ goes through food. Number 1, the guy looks like he doesn't fit in. He got the beard and the Harvard look and you have to wonder if this white guy can handle us girls. I mean he looks like he should be teaching somewhere up the hills or what Chester always calls JFK's kids and not with us losers. I give him about two weeks before these girls drive him crazy. Still I watched him when he came into the school today for his interview and he didn't look too put off by the crazies. I give him a week and then we will see. Again, the odds are in my favor he leaves.

At precisely 6:30 p.m., Anthony Romero appeared in the school's kitchen with three very large grocery bags filled with a variety of ingredients for his "demonstration pizza lesson."

Mrs. T. greeted him with a curious facial expression.

"Ahhhhhhhhh," Mrs. T. asked, "I thought you were supposed to do a demonstration school lesson? Looks like you are about to start a pizzeria instead? What gives? I mean, if this is your demonstration school lesson, well, you'll have to do some explaining to Chester or Mr. Harvard man.

He is all about academics . . . the Harvard man! Actually, didn't you go there too?"

Anthony only nodded his head.

"Let's see now," said Mrs. T. "We have Chester, Toni, Michael the new counselor, and if you're hired we can start calling this academy . . . Harvard West, or how about the Harvard Project? Sounds way too important?"

"The way to these girl's brains will be through their bodies," said Anthony, unpacking the grocery bags, specifically their stomachs. My lesson requires them to read a recipe, measure, as in math, determine caloric intake, cooperate and communicate with others or social skills, follow directions and more reading, learn about cooking temperature or the science of cooking, and so forth. Bottom line: attach their kinesthetic intelligence to their emotions, which is physical, and most of all the lesson tastes good!"

Mrs. T. flashed a questioning look and said nothing.

"Well, pizza should get their attention," she said. "I'll drink or eat to that. But I get what you are saying, but you cannot teach them by reading pizza recipes or learn science as in cooking and what did you say . . . caloric intake or something like that?"

"Yes and no," said Anthony. "You have to show them that they need to learn how to read to survive in this world. Learning how to cook, you need to be able to read. I am just trying to connect their love for food with reading and school."

"You'll have to convince Chester about your new way of teaching these girls," she offered with a smile. "He is a hard nut to crack, as you have already learned."

"Ok, let's get started," he interrupted, emptying the last shopping bag. "We can talk about that later. Maybe you can help with prepping the lesson?"

Mrs. T. jumped up enthusiastically, rubbing her hands together, and said, "Just show me what you want me to do. Hey, already I like your style and they get to eat the lesson too, which will be a first. The girls will love that, especially DJ. The poor girl got a serious food problem, which spells overweight. She won't let anyone weigh her but she has to be close to 400 pounds. Poor thing."

"Perhaps her love of food is her need to be loved." returned Anthony.

"We had to put locks on the refrigerator and cabinets because they steal food like it's money," she explained, unpacking the bags. "Maybe with a real teacher/principal these girls will feel better about themselves instead of feeding their problems with junk food."

Anthony opened a pizza ingredients package and began explaining the lesson.

"We will go with three stations. One station will be for cutting the veggies and sausage. Also, we will make one pizza for those who are vegetarians. Another station will be for rolling out the dough. I cheated with store-bought dough because of the time factor; I did not have time to let it sit overnight. Another station will take care of the sauce and the grating of cheese."

Mrs. T. nodded her head and followed Anthony's every direction.

"Check this out," said Anthony pulling out a red and white checkered tablecloth. "I brought in these tablecloths like the ones you see in traditional Italian restaurants and even some old Chianti bottles. We can put candles in the bottles to make it look like the real thing. I even have some Italian music by Dean Martin!"

Mrs. T. watched and listened, occasionally getting wide-eyed or just nodding her head, impressed by Anthony's potential cooking lesson.

"I need one big thing," he continued. "Can we use the card tables you have been using for school?"

"No problem," she said. Then Mrs. T. began to sing, "When the moon hits your eye like a big pizza pie, that's amore!"

Minutes later a few girls appeared in the kitchen, wondering what the demonstration lesson would be.

"Hallelujah!" shouted DJ seeing the preparations. "I thought we were going to get a headache doing math or English, but I think I'm goin' to like this Romeo dude. You know I can't function without my grunts. It's in my psyche evaluation. DJ needs food to be nice and smart."

"Like in smart ass," returned Mrs. T.

The rest of the girls appeared in the kitchen and immediately started pumping Mrs. T. about Anthony's cooking lesson.

"A pizza-cooking lesson?" challenged Kim. "You really think Chester's going to go for a pizza-cooking lesson? Oh, well. I think we will begin to call this guy the one-and-done man!"

Thirty minutes later, all the pizza-preparation stations were set up.

"Remember," Anthony explained, "there will not be any pizza unless you make it."

"Whoa," said DJ falling down into a chair. "I don't make pizza, I buy it and then eat it. Why not just fake it? I mean there's good place down the street that does good take out."

"Yeah," seconded Kim, "I'll eat to that."

"Mr. Anthony don't play," interrupted Mrs. T. "His cooking lesson will help you with school and learning, like how to measure the ingredients that go into the pizza. That's right, girl. If you want to eat, then you got make it, and you can take that to your stomach!"

"Not sure if pizza man is all there," replied Tina. "I thought this guy is supposed to help us pass the GED, not learning how to make stupid pizzas. We go from no teachers to a pizza man who does cookin' classes instead of math and English. This is bullshit!"

"Why make Italian food? "suggested Kim. "I mean we should be eating ribs, mashed potatoes, you know, soul food!"

"Nobody is ignoring your wishes," returned Anthony. "We can do another cooking class, and we can go for ribs."

He stopped and waited for a response but since no one stepped up he returned to his pizza lesson.

"Your names are listed with the different prep stations. One station will grate mozzarella and parmesan cheese. Another station will cut up the sausage and vegies. Another station will make the dough, which is store-bought, but you still must cut it up and spread it out. Another station will do set-up. I wrote down the exact ingredients of all the food that will go into making the pizza as well as the calories, fat, and so forth. Do you know that one slice of cheese pizza contains 410 calories, 14 grams of fat, 8 grams of saturated fat, and 780 milligrams of cholesterol? Add with pepperoni and you get 480 calories, 20 grams of fat, 9 grams of saturated fat, and 980 milligrams of sodium."

They all looked at DJ, who just threw up her hands and yelled, "Why is everyone looking at me? I need more calories because . . . well, I'm bigger than all you pussies!"

"Here are more facts: teens with little or no exercise," Anthony continued, "need about 1,600 calories a day and teenage girls with moderate exercise about 2,200 calories—that's if you weight about 125 pounds. After we are through with the meal, we will run numbers for whatever we added to make the pizzas and compare it to what the experts say is a wholesome meal . . . basic math, which you will need for the GED."

Anthony took out a bowl and had the girls pick out their assignments for the stations.

"I get to pick first because I'm the hungriest and biggest?" yelled DJ. "She pulled out a piece of paper that said, "Grate cheese, station 1."

DJ moved to her station and began to dance around until she broke a nail.

"God damn," she screamed looking at Anthony. "Now whose goin' to pay for my next manicure?"

"I get to cut up the veggies," read Denise. "Oh, well . . . so much for my nails."

"I get to make the dough and I not talking about money," added Jewels, trying to fit in.

"Enough with your corny jokes," reprimanded Charlene. "Just do your damn job!"

JEWELS ODOM COMMENTARY #8

The girls have yet to accept me because I refuse to dress in their ghetto Halloween costumes. I wear running pants, top, and running shoes, which really pisses them off because they say I'm being uppity or dress like an Oreo or valley girl. Unless these girls make the change from ghetto head to GED head, they will always be facing an uphill battle.

Ten minutes later, the girls were all paired up and moved to their stations. Mr. T. walked around like the Gestapo making sure no one ate any of the food preparations.

"Making the dough is always difficult," reminded Anthony. "Remember, the dough is the base for everything else to go on top of. Again, you should make the dough the night before and then let it sit in the fridge overnight, so it can rise. We have to cheat a little and buy store dough." Surprisingly, the students all remained silent, listening to Anthony, with the exception of DJ, who twisted a long piece of cheese and pretended to use it like a mustache.

"That's a warning missy," intervened Mrs. T. "The next time you can take it up with Chef Chester!"

"Just tryin' to look like that gay guy on the pizza box," she defended. "Chef boy are you stupid looking or whatever!"

Anthony ignored DJ and explained, "Whatever station you are at, you need to choose one person who is the recorder of the number of calories, fats, and so on, based on quantity and so forth. Usually on the back of the item you will have the number of calories, fats, and so on. If not, you got to look up the calories in this book that I brought in that defines food intake and calories with the pizza ingredients you will use today."

About thirty minutes later, three large pizzas were completed with little or no fanfare. Only DJ was caught eating cheese, which made Mrs. T. stand so close to her that DJ complained, "She is taking all my oxygen. If I can't breathe, I can't eat!"

"Girl, then hold your breath!"

"I am supposed to grate the cheese," DJ said, ignoring Mrs. T., "which makes me the big cheese so cut me some slack."

"It will take about forty-five minutes before they are all cooked," said Anthony, checking out the three large pizzas in the oven. While they waited, Anthony decided they would clean up the kitchen.

During clean-up, DJ began to playfully throw a leftover piece of dough at Kim.

"What the hell?!" yelled Kim, pulling the dough out of her hair. "Hey, somebody is throwing dough around and it landed in my freaking hair!"

"If I catch anyone throwing dough," warned Mrs. T., "they will have to answer to me!"

When Mrs. T. turned her back, Tina threw flour at Kim, making her black hair turn white.

"No way," Kim screamed. "What's your problem, girl? I knew it was you because you got flour all over your hands!"

Kim responded by angrily throwing flour back at Tina. Instead the flour hit DJ in the face.

"Hey, look at DJ!" yelled Kim. "I always knew she was a honky!"

DJ responded by throwing flour back at Tina, but the flour hit Jewels, and then the cooking class erupted into one huge flour and dough fight with all the girls throwing flour and dough in every direction. Even Anthony got hit in the face.

When Mrs. T. put up her hands to stop, she got hit with dough as well, so she automatically threw dough back at the girls. The flour and dough fight lasted about five minutes, until Chester and Toni appeared in the doorway.

Chester looked at the condition of the kitchen and all the students, Mrs. T., and Anthony covered in flour and dough.

"Anthony . . . when you said you were doing a cooking lesson, you really meant it," said Chester, munching on a piece of green pepper. "Oh well," he added, "as long it's a learning experience. Ain't that right, honey?"

Toni just smiled and said, "*Bon appétit* . . . when do we eat? But first," she added, "I want to stay out of this war zone until you all clean yourselves and the kitchen. Isn't that right, ladies?"

After clean-up, Chester and Toni sat down with the girls, while Tina, Jewels, and Denise began serving three large pizzas to the music of Dean Martin and candle light.

"Slow feet don't eat!" screamed DJ racing to the table.

About thirty minutes later, after the pizzas had been eaten, Chester and Anthony went out to the front porch to the music of Dean Martin and the chorus of girls singing very loudly, "When the moon hits your eye like a big pizza pie, that's amore!"

"Well, you convinced me that you can make pizza," said Chester. "The million-dollar question is: Can you get the natives to pass the GED? And, if so, can you start tomorrow at 7:30 a.m.? I will have a contract drawn up, and you can sign it tomorrow. My handshake is always good. Isn't that right dear?"

"Get it in writing," warned Toni. "I am still waiting for that diamond you promised me!"

Chester turned to Anthony and asked, "Are you married?"

"No . . . um, not at this time."

"Good! Maybe you will last till June."

Toni slapped Chester across the back.

"Why did you do that?"

Toni walked away singing, "Don't know much about Algebra. Don't know much about geometry . . . !"

Chester took a deep breath and sighed. "One last thing," he said seriously, "I want you to read the girls' files ASAP. Ask Toni for them. They are in my office. You need to know just what you're getting into. You do have life insurance and you aren't married, but do have a girlfriend?"

Anthony laughed and said almost apologetically: "Yes to the first and no to the second, but I do have a girlfriend."

"Well, Chester responded, "You got about two-thirds right!"

JEWELS ODOM COMMENTARY #9

You didn't have to be a brain scientist to figure out that food is a big deal with us girls. Anthony is Italian through and through. They say Italians have this thing about food—like food is almost a religious experience to them—so it made sense that if you are going to get abused street girls to trust you, then why not feed them?

The following day at approximately 7:30 a.m., Mrs. T. appeared from a side entrance of the old mansion-turned-school.

"You're here early," she said, perplexed. "Oh well, you know what they say: the early bird catches the worm, or this man ain't foolin' around!" She raised her hand for a high five and Anthony slapped it hard.

Mrs. T. was a widower who began working at the Clark Academy when it first opened about three months ago. She started as an aide at Chester's and Toni's Queen Street School for students age 11–16, located a few miles from the Clark Academy. However, she was transferred to the day shift at the Clark Academy because she had been around the block and knew the ins and outs of the Oakland and San Francisco mean streets when and if Chester and the girls took to the streets for field trips. She could walk the walk. "Mrs. T. plays no games and you can take that to the bank" was her favorite saying, although, as you will read, based on her mood, on occasion, she inserted other words for *bank*, or added other words for effect. She drove a beat-up 1958 white Eldorado convertible that was always on display when she left school each day. The girls would rush out to the front porch hooting and hollering for her to burn rubber, and she never disappointed her onlookers. With the broken muffler and a beat-up bomb of a car, she would tease the girls by starting off slowly, and at the last minute she would floor it and tear down the street with a loud blast from the engine and squealing tires, much to the delight of the girls, but not so with the neighbors. This lasted about a week at best, until the neighbors complained and Chester quickly put an end to Mrs. T.'s Grand Prix delusions!

"They won't be down till 8:30," she yelled to herself. "Hallelujah! I couldn't keep them under control for a whole day when there is no sub-teacher. Not right hiring one sub, then another sub, or when the subs get fed up with the girls and call in sick and never come back again!"

"I have to raise the large picture window so I can throw out all the junk furniture," proposed Anthony.

Miraculously, Juan, the school's custodian, appeared and asked Anthony if he needed help. He looked at Anthony attempting to open the window and said, "You know it hasn't been open in years."

"I was afraid I would break the frame and glass," he said rubbing his fingers along the window pane.

"Let me go and get a crowbar and that should get it open," said Juan, rushing out of the room.

Juan returned with a crowbar and carefully placed the crowbar under the fragile window pane and began to gently pry the window open. After a few hard pushes, the window opened.

"Well," said Mrs. T, peeking into the room, "it's about time somebody opened that window! It's been years since a breath of fresh air came through. Finally, this old lady will be able to breathe!"

Juan took the crowbar and wedged it under the window again, while Anthony plied his fingers under the window pane.

"One, two, three . . . push," ordered Anthony, but the window barely moved up a few inches. However, they were more successful on the second try and created a three-foot opening.

"Yessssssss!" screamed Mrs. T. "Yesssssss! She can breathe! Halleluiah! Praise the Lord!"

Once the window was open, Anthony began to throw furniture out the large window opening like a remodeler ready to refit a house. With each piece of discarded furniture, there was a loud crash.

His jubilant tossing continued until Jewels, DJ, and Kim appeared in the living room dressed in bathrobes carrying baseball bats and brooms.

"We thought you were some weirdo breaking in," explained DJ. "Still, it would have been nice if he were a man like Prince." DJ stopped and thought and yelled out, "Prince, do you hear me!"

"There's going to be big trouble when Chester sees all his good furniture thrown out," warned Kim with bug eyes. "This furniture is really valuable."

"Oh yeah, like valuable to junk dealers," declared Mrs. T., holding back her laughter.

The girls left for the upstairs but not without banging their shoes loudly on the stairs like gunfire.

Anthony was new to the school, but he did notice the girls' habit of how they expressed their anger. Angel would speak Spanish when angry; for others, it was their shoes banging on the wooden stairs that sounded like gunfire, which he was always thankful that it was only the girls' shoes.

Once the junk furniture had been thrown out, only a rolled-up large rug sat in the middle of the room like a beached whale.

"We'll wait until the girls return," said Anthony. "They need to take ownership for their new classroom.

"I'll drink to that," said Mrs. T., taking a sip from her coffee cup.

Fifteen minutes later the girls reappeared to greet Anthony, who was sitting on the rolled-up rug surrounded by several buckets of water, sponges, and rags.

The girls were dressed in their usual "street-walking" uniforms; black, tight-fitting leather pants, low halter tops, black high-heel shoes, lots of make-up, and teased hair, which said they were clearly not ready for Anthony's next assignment—cleaning the classroom walls.

JEWELS ODOM COMMENTARY #10

As I said earlier, how we dress and how we look at life is going to be one of the greatest challenges Anthony will face. Again, once he gets the "make believe" classroom together his next challenge will be changing our street or ghetto identity to a learning identity. Stay tuned!

"I should have warned you," said Anthony to now fourteen indignant girls who stood off to the side wondering what their new "teacher director man" had in mind.

"You cannot have a school unless you have a classroom. They sort of go hand in hand."

"What?! "screamed Tina. "We like our school the way it is. We could study on the couch or floor. We could study when we want to. You know nice and laid back. What we all like, ain't that right, girls?"

Standing in the hallway looking like a bouncer with arms folded was Mrs. T., who responded loudly: "Rule number 1 . . . in life, whenever a man, especially a Harvard man, wants to build you a classroom, a school, a home, a garage, a classroom, whatever, you let the man on the floor do it. Comprendo or whatever?"

They all shot daggers at Mrs. T., who refused to give up her imitation of "shop bully."

"Rule number 2," continued Mrs. T., "is to get your sad-looking booties up to your rooms and change your clothes. The man on the floor said you got to build a classroom, which means we got to clean the classroom. Anyone not down here in ten minutes will get written up and you can take that to the bank, and even Mr. Clean!"

They reluctantly left for the upstairs with much talking under their breath and, of course, deliberately expressing their anger with their high heels on the wooden stairs, but this time it was only a slow round of gunfire.

Right on time they appeared in jeans or sweatpants, T-shirts, no bras, and so on, to DJ's announcement: "No judge ever said I was goin' to do hard labor, so how about hardly labor?"

First, Anthony demonstrated how to wash the walls with soapy water and a sponge.

"She's been here for years and nobody ever gave her a make-over," he described, waving his arms like an artist about to begin a new creation. "Those who want to do the walls, please take a sponge and start washing. Those who want to sweep can sweep. Leftover workers can join the other workers."

Denise started sweeping the floor, while Jewels and Kim washed walls. Everything was going smoothly when Patricia found a dead mouse in the closet and decided to chase the girls around the old mansion like they were escaping a T. Rex. Finally, Patricia discarded the dead mouse in the trashcan so everyone could ever go back into "that damn rat-filled-hole school!"

The girls return to their work stations, but Patricia was not finished with her mouse caper and appeared again with a black sock, which caused the girls to start escaping again, until they realized it was only a black sock.

Normalcy returned to cleaning the classroom, or until Tina broke a nail.

"God damn it! I Just broke my fuckin' nail. Now whose goin' to pay for my pedicure?"

"I'm writing you up for using the F-bomb!" roared Mrs. T., jotting down Tina's name in her little black book.

"You tellin' me that if you broke a nail you wouldn't be pissed off!" Tina screamed.

Mrs. T walked away whistling. "Whistle while you work!"

Next, Anthony needed help shoving the large rolled-up rug through the picture window. He left for the outside and in minutes he was at the window asking the girls to push while he pulled, but the girls could barely budge the rug a few feet.

"Everyone outta the way!" screamed DJ. "Out of my way, cuz DJ is a comin'!"

DJ backed up several feet and charged the rug like a wild bull and all 400 pounds slammed into the rug and the rug flew through the window. She fell on the floor in a heap. Then the rest of the girls piled on top of her laughing, hugging, and giggling, until Tina yelled, "N****r pile!"

"Girl," yelled Kim, "if I hear you use that word again, I am goin' to smack you across the head and then some!"

Tina responded, "Well . . . sorry."

"Okay," intervened Jewels, "let's move on."

"Excuse me!" yelled Anthony from the outside, "when you finish with your fun, help get this thing off me!"

DJ peered out of the window and announced, "You have to take us all to Clint's Barbecue. Yes or no?"

"Okay, now get out here and push the rug off of me!"

For the next two hours, the girls scrubbed the walls, and to Anthony's surprise, they actually became cleaning professionals, but not without the help of Stevie Wonder, Michael Jackson, Prince, Marvin Gaye, and whatever music they played and gyrated to.

For lunch, Anthony ordered three large pizzas, which only made the experience more positive.

After lunch, Anthony announced their next labor of love was a trip to a local lumber yard.

"Ohhhhh me!" cried Kim. "I think I'm going to like this field trip. Men with muscles and stuff!"

With Anthony's announcement, the girls raced back upstairs for costume change number 2.

The ritual banging of shoes on the stairs evoked only a semi-automatic-like pistol sound instead of machine-gun-like anger.

Mrs. T. presented the wisest response to Anthony: "Thou shall never announce a field trip because they become like gone as in *Gone With the Wind*, and now you are part of a real live movie."

JEWELS ODOM COMMENTARY #11

As I said earlier, how we dress and how we look at life is going to be one of the greatest challenges Anthony will face. Again, once he gets the classroom together, his next challenge will be changing our street or ghetto identity to a learning identity.

At approximately 2:30 p.m., Anthony Romero led fourteen (so-called) highly promiscuous love-starved street girls across a Berkeley lumberyard parking lot. At approximately 2:31 p.m., the male lumberyard employees and customers immediately became mesmerized by the strange sight of fourteen adolescent girls in tight-fitting, black leather pants, black halter tops, and black high-heel boots heading in the direction of the Berkeley Lumber Company's front door.

Immediately, two male employees responded like they had just won the lottery with attitudes that their work was no longer going to be work!

Within seconds, the girls were conveniently met at the lumberyard's front entrance and offered five-star assistance. A quick glance by a forklift operator nearly caused him to drop his load of lumber. Another employee appeared with one piece of lumber in his hand offering his assistance. Anthony divided the girls up into groups and matched them with male employees, who did not attempt to hide their looks of appreciation.

Next, a panicked loudspeaker's voice announced that help was needed up front. In another area of the store, two employees demonstrated for Tina, Kim, and DJ how to hammer, saw, and sand while the rest of the girls were shown how to paint and stain.

After the loudspeaker announced for the third time, "Please . . . help is needed up front," the lumberyard workers moved swiftly to other areas of the store to support customers, but not without shaking all the girls' hands and wishing them good luck in the building of their new school.

JEWELS ODOM COMMENTARY #12

On our return trip to school, we stopped at a red light in front of a local public high school. Crowds of students were standing on the sidewalk, talking or just celebrating that the school day had ended.

For us girls, something very strange happened. Instead of hiding under their seats, embarrassed that they were riding in a broken-down yellow school bus, they all stayed upright in their seats, and some of the girls actually waved to the "cuties" or the boys who were standing on the sidewalk.

When we returned to school, the girls had a certain air of confidence. Maybe, just maybe, they realized that hammering, sanding, and so on, could be more effective without all the tight-fitting clothing, high heels, and so forth. Bottom line, it was a win-win situation for all involved. Also, we realized that we could just be normal with men, and for the men, they became teachers to us girls. Maybe this is why we didn't freak out when we stopped in front of the school.

It was late afternoon when Mrs. T. heard a knock on the mansion's back door. Standing alone was an older gray-haired black man about sixty-five years old named Mr. Joseph.

"I'm from the lumberyard," he said softly. "I am here to deliver a can of stain, brushes, paint thinner, and wood."

"Welcome, Mr. Joseph. I'm Mrs. T., the school's line counselor," she said, impressed by the gentle nature of Mr. Joseph. "I will get Mr. Romero, our school principal, to help you."

Anthony appeared and explained why he needed the stain and the rest of the supplies.

"I want to try and restore some of the walnut walls with clear stain," he said. "Bring this old lady back to life. We have cleaned the walls the best we could, but now comes the make-up!"

Mr. Joseph looked at Anthony with apprehension and then at the girls and said, "Let me get the stain from my truck."

Anthony followed Mr. Joseph to his truck and helped bring the materials to the back door of the old mansion.

"If you have the time I would like to show you our project," explained Anthony. In the back of Anthony's mind were several possibilities. First, Mr. Joseph was a black man with a gentle voice, but also, he would know more about staining than Anthony, which could become a teaching moment for the girls.

Mr. Joseph followed Anthony into the new classroom, and Mr. Joseph immediately began to examine the walnut wooden walls like a surgeon about to begin a major operation.

The girls stood off in the distance, watching Mr. Joseph suspiciously.

"This wood is really beautiful," he said, running his hands over the rich walnut walls. "You don't see this kind of woodwork in homes to-day—too expensive. But this is something else."

"Easy there, Mr. Delivery Man," said DJ. "That's my blood, sweat, and tears as in cleaning the walls."

He turned to Anthony and the girls and said in a serious tone, "First, you need to put this stain on gently like make-up on a young woman's face. You don't want to hide her beautiful skin." He looked at Patricia and said, "Like this child. I mean, I don't want to offend you, little lady, but you know if you got too much make-up on, it will prevent the skin from breathing. The same for this wood."

Patricia only blushed and remained quiet.

"You got that right, Mr. Joseph," interrupted Mrs. T. "I keep tellin' these girls that a little bit goes a long way, but they don't listen. They keep playin' 'Hush Hush Sweet Charlotte' with all that make-up!"

Mr. Joseph smiled and opened a can of clear stain and began to carefully apply the stain to the walls with a brush.

"It needs to go like this," he demonstrated. "No rushing. Just take your time with smooth strokes, so you don't streak the old lady to death."

Four girls started staining the walls while Mr. Joseph watched with careful eyes.

"Are you girls sure you never stained wood before?" he asked, then commented with smile, "already you are experts . . . artists."

"After we finish the walls, we need to start building bookcases and bulletin boards for the classroom," explained Anthony, concerned.

"I would like to offer my help," said Mr. Joseph, checking his watch. "I am way ahead of my schedule today. If you want my help, that is."

"Really?" questioned Anthony, enthused. "Thank you so much. I will work with these girls building bookcases and maybe you can continue on the walls?"

Anthony had the four girls measure wood for the bookcases and bulletin boards, and Mr. Joseph started on the walls with the rest of the class.

JEWELS ODOM COMMENTARY #13

This old dude, Mr. Joseph, with his gentle voice and kind face, helped us see how beautiful our school or "make believe" classroom could really be, and maybe ourselves as well. Also, he was a black man and not the usual black, brown, or white Man on the Floor who wanted to take something from us, but he was a man who came across with a sense of sincerity and respect, something that we were not use to in our life. You have to understand that we never really had men that we could trust or someone who treated us like their own.

After Mr. Joseph left, all we talked about was "Mr. Joseph this" and "Mr. Joseph that" and what kind of life we would have had if we had a father, an uncle, or any black man that treated us with respect. I think Anthony saw this when Mr. Joseph suggested to stay a bit and help us with our school. We all hoped that Mr. Joseph would come back again because for the short time he was around, I know we all felt a sense of respect and not worthlessness but proud of being just us.

FOUR

Used Desks

Anthony didn't know what he was (really) getting into when he called the San Francisco Unified School District warehouse for used desks. A man with a very gruff, no-nonsense voice stated that they had desks of all sizes, and anything else we needed for a school.

Anthony and six girls piled into their school bus and headed over to San Francisco. The trip took longer than he had expected because Anthony had to drive around numerous streets to find the old warehouse located in what the girls referred to as "ghetto and gang banger land . . . a place you never go at night unless you are with your pimp or gang bangers!"

They pulled up to a very large, thick metal warehouse. A small sign was screwed to the door that read *S.F.U.S.D.—No Trespassing*. Anthony pushed an intercom-like button, and within seconds, the same suspicious, gruff voice he had heard on the phone grumbled, "This is John. What do you want?"

"I called earlier," returned Anthony tentatively. "We are here from the Clark Academy. We need to buy used desks."

"I will be at the warehouse door in a few minutes," growled the voice.

"I get weird vibes about this place," said Angel, "especially when I hear Mr. Weirdo's voice. I ain't goin' in there unless I have a gun." She punctuated her fear in Spanish and mumbled, "*Peligro!*"

"Yeah, a gun," whispered Kim sarcastically. "Oh yeah, I always carry one whenever we go on field trips, just for weirdos like him. Hello?"

JEWELS ODOM COMMENTARY #14

I noticed that Anthony often looks at me for advice or approval when dealing with the girls. I don't want the girls to think I am trying to get on his good side, but this guy often asks me for directions when making a serious move with us girls like turning him on to the S.F.U.S.D. warehouse. The place was in a bad area where I often went to buy drugs. I never really paid any serious attention to the old warehouse building until Anthony mentioned he needed desks. I suggested, and he followed through. Still, the warehouse was in a neighborhood you didn't want to hang out in without your homeboys.

It is important for this school to succeed because if they close it down, we could all end up back at the hall or CYA. Also, how about all the girls at the hall who need a program like this? So, I figure I will help him the best I can without taking sides, if you get my drift.

Minutes later, the metal door screeched open, and a strange-looking man named John appeared. He was tall, hunched over, with long hair and a beard.

Kim whispered, "Ahhhhhh, is this a remake of the movie *The Thing*?"

"Shiiiiit," warned Tina. "We may never get out of this place."

"I believe you are looking for some desks," he said, sizing up Anthony and his female contingent. "Follow me, and don't get lost!"

Cautiously, they followed John into the dark, damp graveyard of discarded school furniture.

Their senses were immediately attacked with the intense smell of mold and whatever had died in the place.

"Mister John," said DJ, "I'll give you a dollar for an oxygen mask. The smell is killing me."

"Like every day," he said, annoyed, "so get used to it!"

"Maybe every day, I would call 911," she returned, holding her nose.

"Whatever desks you could find, you can have for ten bucks each," offered John, walking away. "Just holler when you find some desks."

After John left the Clark Academy contingency, there was complete quiet among the girls, who looked at each other with fear.

"I knew I should have left a note with Mrs. T.," declared Tina. "If not back in two hours, call police!"

They continued to walk carefully through the dark, cold storage warehouse filled with the past skeletons of school desks, chairs, filing cabinets, and of course, the many spiders that reminded the girls they should never deviate from the narrow warehouse pathway. After walking around in the dark, cold warehouse for about 30 minutes, they finally found some old drafting desks that were in good shape.

Anthony and the girls sang out with one loud "John! We need you!"

In minutes, John appeared from somewhere.

"They don't make desks like this anymore," he said proudly. "These desks are indestructible."

While John and another coworker loaded the fourteen drafting desks onto the school bus, John began to talk seriously about the desks almost as if they were his children.

"You may think of these desks as junk, but they belonged to unusual students like yourselves. Today, some might be architects, teachers, or even a criminal or two. Just remember, they sat in these desks, and their legacy could be yours as well."

The girls were stunned by John's eulogy about the desks and only stared in disbelief.

"Good luck," he stated sincerely with a smile. "Good luck. I hope you all do well in school."

JEWELS ODOM COMMENTARY #15

When John spoke about the many students who sat in the same desks we were purchasing, the sincerity of his lecture shook all of us. At first, he was the grim reaper and then a wise lecturer, and a very sincere man, making a deep connection with us. His speech meant a great deal, because he was the Man on the Floor showing his deep feelings about some old, discarded desks that no one really cared about, yet attempting to help street kids move on in their lives. Personally, I felt like he was speaking directly to each one of us who were like the beat-up desks that no one really cared about—discarded, left alone in a cold, old warehouse. Was Anthony giving us experiences like this, and another view of the world, or another image of the Man on the Floor for us to forgive?

There was very little space in the bus for the girls to sit down, so a few of us had to sit on the floor, which DJ made sure Anthony was aware of, letting everyone know that she was not about to let this personal sacrifice go unnoticed.

Throughout the ride, they brought up creepy John's short speech about the desks. Jewels set the record straight. "John wasn't creepy at all. It meant a lot that we were buying his desks to become emancipated."

"Shut up! He still was creepy," replied Kim. "If you like him so much, I can call him and set up a date for you!"

Once they returned to the school and carried the heavy engineering desks into the classroom, the next challenge was to clean up the old desks.

First, the girls washed the desktops, getting off all the dirt and grime that had accumulated over the years. The cleaning brought out all sorts of interesting comments about the carvings from the interior of the desks.

"Hey! Check out this one!" yelled Tina. "For a good hand job call Terry at 327-8456."

"I have a better one," said Charlene. "For good head, meet me outside in the back of the gym at noon on Tuesdays only."

"Whoa," said DJ, "this girl is organized as well as horny. I wonder how old and where she is now. When we get back, let's call her."

"Oh yeah," suggested Tina. "Maybe she'll answer from the cemetery, like six feet down!"

After the girls finished cleaning the inside and outside of their desks and staining the wood tops, it took about sixty minutes for the desks to dry.

It was early evening when Kathleen, on the 3–11 p.m. line staff, called Anthony at his home.

"I have a serious dilemma that I need you to solve," stated Kathleen in a very concerned voice.

Anthony turned to his girlfriend, Madison, with a panic expression and thought to himself, *Someone has been shot or arrested!*

He took a deep breath and waited for Kathleen to finish her statement.

"The girls want to eat their dinners at their desks. I told them no food is allowed in the classroom."

"That's great," returned Anthony, holding back his excitement. "I think it is wonderful that they feel they have a place of their own to go to. No problem. Let them eat at their desks."

Anthony hung up the phone and walked slowly over to Madison and gave her the longest embrace. Neither said a word for the longest time.

"They always say that no news is good news," commented Madison. "Well this is a time when they were wrong."

After the girls had finished their dinner and chores, they appeared in their pajamas and sat at their desks, writing letters and reading.

Kathleen called Anthony again. "I can't believe what I am seeing," she said, whispering into the phone. "They are still at their desks and they want to stay up later than curfew to continue reading or writing letters to friends. Well," she continued. "maybe the smell of the desks has gone to their heads because I don't believe in miracles!"

"Give them an extra thirty minutes," said Anthony. "Good night and great job!"

FIVE

Maya Angelou to the Rescue

You didn't have to be a rocket scientist to realize the girls' academic skills were seriously below grade level. In fact, if you completed a composite of the reading levels of the fourteen girls, the average girl would be lucky to test out at a fifth-grade level.

Since Anthony had been hired as the teacher/principal, he had spent each day after school examining the thick files of the girls, reflecting on their educational and psychological history from years of moving in and out of various residential schools and county school programs.

Moreover, from their many years in foster care, residential school programs, juvie, and of course the Oakland/San Francisco streets, the little time they had spent in school had only exacerbated the students' serious learning disabilities and weak reading skills, both cognitively and emotionally. Without the consistency of developmental reading programs, children not only fall behind but also develop a negative perception toward reading that can be lifelong. Lastly, including the biological manifestations—such as FAS (fetal alcohol syndrome), maternal drug addiction, and physical and emotional abandonment—their so-called "learning brains" could have been permanently damaged.

Anthony carefully examined each file while dealing with a teacher's fear that maybe aiming to improve their reading skills as well as pass the GED was too much to expect of the girls and of himself. He stood up and walked around the small office, trying to gain a sense of focus about how to improve the girls' weak reading skills, which were further exacerbated by the teenage resistance to reading. He gazed out the window into the glow of the setting sun, looking for some hope, and for a brief moment, the sun's warm rays seemed like a good sign until his day-dreaming was quickly disturbed by the girls' loud music that blasted from the outside porch, feeding their dance-frenzied bodies and arguments over the use of the pay phone.

It was obvious he needed to address the girls' lack of interest in reading. He debated with himself. *If I could help them read with some degree of fluency and comprehension, they just might pass the GED and even develop a love of reading.*

Nevertheless, at that time, their main interests in reading were *Us* and *People* magazines and some reading matter that Toni brought in about programs catering to black youth, which sat on a bookcase gathering dust. Further, when they did read the magazines, they only *capped on* the celebrities who frequented the pages with rude and condescending comments: "Who spends lots of money on their bodies to stay younger like mostly rich, white honkies?"

However, Anthony stared intensely at the box of books that sat on his desk that could be the magical cure to opening up the girls' need to improve their reading skills. He needed to first lower their reading challenges or fears by making the reading program non-academic. Instead, he would simply call the reading program "Reading for Pleasure."

Anthony's plan was simply to meet as a group once a week for an hour. He would read aloud from the book as well as allowing any other students to volunteer and follow his lead. He would make coffee, hot chocolate, and add in cookies, making the reading class held in the large study room more relaxed and hopefully less threatening. At the completion of each chapter, they would discuss the book's storyline.

The magical book to support the "Reading for Pleasure" experience was the famous autobiographical book by black author and poet Maya Angelou "I Know Why the Caged Bird Sings" and her famous poem of the same name. Anthony truly believed a book about the life of a young black girl growing up in the racist South could raise the interest of the girls to levels that might place them in Maya Angelou's shoes.

For example, as a child, Maya Angelou was moved from caregiver to caregiver, a condition in her life that could connect with the lives of the Clark Academy girls, who had moved from foster home to foster home or residential treatment programs, the streets, and so on. Furthermore, Maya Angelou was tragically raped at seven years of age, which had caused her so much trauma that she had stopped speaking for several years. This traumatic period was the result of being forced by her father to reveal the rapist's name. The act of speaking the man's name was viewed by her as the cause of the man's death. She then refused to speak for several years after his murder.

Throughout her story, the issue of growing up among the blatant racism of the South only sealed her consistent trauma associated with her rape, which some of the Clark Academy girls could also identify with. Other similarities existed between Maya Angelou's and the girls' past histories, numerous residential treatment programs, and even Maya Angelou's teen pregnancy, an experience of some of the Clark Academy girls.

Finally, connecting a reading experience both physically, emotionally, and cognitively through this experience of Maya Angelou's could lead to more than a purely academic perception, serving also as a pathway to understanding their own traumatic lives. Maya Angelou could thus become a role model for the girls.

JEWELS ODOM COMMENTARY #16

Anthony passed out a new book today to support what he called his "Reading for Pleasure" group or class. I think it will help get the girls to start reading a real book instead of all those stupid magazines that only gets them pissed off at all the white women who spend lots of money on their bodies. When he passed the book out, I already knew all about Maya Angelou and her famous book. I think I always wanted to read the book but never had the chance because of the craziness of my life. Anyways, when I got the book, I went right up to my bedroom and started reading it. I couldn't put it down and even got a flashlight to read under my covers, pissing off Angel to no end. Still, if Anthony wants to get us to read, I think he hit the mark for the girls. Thank you, Anthony and Maya Angelou, for giving us hope.

SIX

Constitution Convention

The students found their "special spots" in the living room/study hall: some on the floor, others on chairs, still others on windowsills, and the smart ones or smokers, close to the doors in order to escape if they needed a smoke or might find it necessary to sneak out for a make-believe bathroom break.

All staff, including county social workers, psychologists, line staff, and so on, sat on chairs among the girls, waiting patiently for Chester, with his usual tardiness, to finally appear. Toni pretended not to be losing her mind, pacing back and forth, as DJ described, "like she's in heat . . . only this is a different kind of heat or the kind that says she's really pissed off!"

At approximately 9:30 a.m., still no Chester. DJ decided to do her version of what the constitutional convention meant to her. She stood up and began dancing and singing, "We get to make the rules! Oh yeah! We get to make the rules, and that means I get to eat all I want like snacks to keep me from gettin' uptight!"

Kim followed and began to imitate DJ, singing a little ditty and shaking her body: "I need more time on weekends, oh yeah, and more allowance . . . oh yeah . . . oh yeah!"

The rest of the girls were not at all that impressed by the two girls' announcements of more freedom; instead, their faces reflected a deep concern that they were going to lose the freedom they already had because, one, they had never trusted Chester, and two, they still didn't trust him.

Patricia was the first to fire a volley at "Mr. Big Shot Chester, who is probably yakking with someone . . . buying or selling furniture and doing his stupid Fred Sanford bit!"

Toni tried to quell the uprising by announcing like a barker at a carnival, "Is everyone ready for some fun? We will only have to do this constitutional convention or make the rules and consequences for your program only once, that is, unless things get out of whack, and then we will have to retool."

The girls didn't respond and only sat quietly, some doing their nails, Kim braiding Patricia's hair, others reading *People* magazines, and still others simply lying on the floor with their eyes closed, until Bonita's snoring got the best of her and Toni shouted, "I want everyone present! There will be no sleeping on the job!"

"Cooooooooome on now," she continued. "Are you ready?" "Come on now," she reiterated, "how many times in your lives do you get to make the rules and consequences for your school or living unit? You all should be stoked!"

"Va a haber un gran problema si el señor Big Shot no se muestra pronto," announced Angel. "And for those who don't speaka da language, it means 'there will be a big problem if Mister Big Shot doesn't show up soon!'" Angel always spoke in Spanish when she was most angry, which, according to the girls, was not fair, because it gave her an out if the staff didn't understand Spanish.

"I speak Spanish," offered Toni. "Just one of my many assets. Now listen up," she continued, "you girls don't get it. You could be making history, but only if you buy into this program. Those who don't . . . well, you know what I always say!"

All the girls sang out loudly, "Yeah . . . and you can take that to the hall!"

"Well, if you want to know what I think," shouted DJ, "Mr. Late is probably over at the Pie Queen havin' a great piece of pie while we sit here waitin' and starvin' to death. I propose we stop this moral development meeting and all head down to Lois's Pie Queen to bust Chester. I mean it will make us more moral. After that we could top it off at Clint's Barbecue for a night cap."

"Well," interrupted Mrs. T., "if it makes you *more moral*, I will personally go down to the Pie Queen after this meeting and get us a few pies, but only if it makes you *more moral*. Praise the Lord!"

"Thank you, Mrs. T., for your so-called *moralosity* . . . if there is such a word," replied Toni with a sardonic smile. "As for Miss DJ," Toni continued, "thank you for your gracious suggestion but we have other fish to fry than pies and ribs, which by the way is your school program, so no Pie Queen or Clint's for now—thank you."

"Just a suggestion from my stomach," DJ muttered while flashing her gold front tooth for affect.

"I know you all think this school is like all the other places you have tried to escape from," continued Toni seriously, "but this school has no walls, no Man on the Floor. One of the reasons why the courts sent you here is because it's a new approach to helping you learn to respect rules, called a Just Community. The courts heard about the Niantic Women's Prison Project's success and since you all have not-so-nice criminal records, they selected you to be a part of this experimental program. After serious prison riots, the warden asked Dr. Kohlberg of Harvard University to help start a Just Community. The key to their success was that they moved the inmates out of their cells and into cottages inside the prison walls . . . and get this," she continued, "they allowed the inmates and prison staff to make the rules and consequences for their living unit."

"The program worked so well that later, they moved the inmates outside the prison and into rooms at a local YMCA. Chester and myself worked on the Niantic Project and decided to start the Queen Street School for eleven- to sixteen-year-olds and ultimately your school for older girls."

"Just because it worked with a bunch of old prisoners doesn't mean it can work here," said DJ, trying to roll over on her side.

"Look at DJ!" yelled Kim. "She's like some walrus who can't roll over . . . all 400 pounds of flesh and whatever else she carries with her!"

DJ simply gave her the finger and said curtly, "This 399-pound walrus will deal with you later."

"No capping on one another," interjected Toni. "You owe DJ an apology."

"Okay," said Kim, trying to be contrite, "I am very sorry for sayin' that DJ looks like a 400-pound walrus when she tries to roll over . . . then, how about a 399-pound overweight seal?!"

"Enough!" yelled Jewels, frustrated. "We're not taking this serious. We don't have any more chances left before we all end up back at the hall and then CYA, and I ain't going to CYA."

"Who put you in charge?" yelled Angel. "You ain't in charge of me . . . you with your zebra look! *Tu eres la problema!*"

"You're saying that when we make up the rules and consequences for our school," interjected Patricia, "we will respect the rules better? Come on . . . at the hall that would never work."

There was complete silence with exception of a few girls who changed their positions on the floor.

"Yes," said Toni. "The Just Community worked because when you have power to make the rules and consequences of your living unit or school, you develop personal ownership with the rules."

"Can you imagine doing this at the hall with Louis?" interrupted Jewels.

"Oh, yeah," said Bonita, "it would put him out of business real fast . . . even make the rules worse!"

"Well," continued Toni, "the Just Community would have protected you from the Man on the Floor because you could have written him up for whatever his wrongs were!"

"Yeah," said DJ, "I'll drink to that. Anyone got a soda?"

"Again, there are few if any programs or schools that support a Just Community philosophy for students with your backgrounds," returned Toni.

"I got to see it to believe it can work," interrupted Kim. "Are you saying we can write up staff if they are unfair or disrespecting us?"

"Yeah," responded Toni, looking around the room for a response.

"Okay," interrupted Kim. "I got a rule right away. Anyone who is late for meetings or whatever needs to be written up!"

"Hello!" yelled DJ. "Chester, you is in deep doo doo!"

"Yeah, since Chester is late!" shouted Kim, "his consequence is to take us all to Clint's Barbecue for dinner!"

"Okay," said Toni seriously, "I agree with you and later we will deal with my not-so-loving husband's tardiness."

"Couch!" shouted DJ. "Couch! Couch!" which got the girls going as they started chanting "Couch! Couch! Couch!"

"Yeah," whispered Tina, "and no nookie for her cookie."

Toni flashed an embarrassed laugh and then looked at her watch and said angrily, "Where is that man? He was late for our wedding. He was even later for our first child. Chester, where the heck are you?"

"And he will be late for his funeral too," protested DJ. "That's if he doesn't get his skinny behind in gear and you can take that to the funeral guy or the couch!"

Moments later, Chester appeared from a side entrance as if he were coming on stage. "Hearrrrrrrrrrrrr Chester . . . the main man is here. Better late than on time, or is it never?"

"Can we get the constitutional convention going?" Toni yelled. "This ain't the *Tonight Show*, you know!"

"More like the *Comedy Hour*," offered Patricia, "or, like I said, 'already I got a rule for being late.'"

The girls all started chanting again, "Couch! Couch! Couch!"

Chester looked over at Toni and shrugged his shoulders. "Am I missing something?"

"We will discuss that later," said Toni.

"You are in deep doo doo," yelled DJ. "And we ain't cleaning it up for Mr. Pie King!"

Again, Chester looked confused.

Custodian Juan appeared with a garbage can and sat it down in the middle of the study hall floor.

"The can is not for your *can* ideas but more like for your *canned* ideas. Get it? *Canned* instead of *can*," joked Chester. "The can is for your bad ideas. I will keep your *can* ideas or good ideas in this bowl for when you write down the consequences to the rules."

Chester stopped for a moment, looked around the room for a response, and continued.

"Okay, I need to read you the rules to the constitutional convention meeting. First, no one talks out of turn; two, you need to raise your hand if you want to speak; three, you are to be respectful to staff and students at all times."

"What am I missing?" asked Chester, looking over at Toni.

"A watch and then some," answered Toni, irritated. "Please, can we get started?"

"Sorry," replied Chester seriously. "Now, let's start with the easy stuff first, like profanity, swearing, wolfing, and so forth."

"Excuse me," interrupted Toni, "first, we need to discuss that profanity or swearing is a habit, or the way some people use certain words more than others like when they're angry. Some use it in everyday speech like *mother 'effin'.'* Some use other types of profanity like *hell* and *damn* and so

forth. I heard DJ and Angel talking the other day and Angel said something really smart, even profound, and DJ said, 'You got to be shittin'
me!' *Shitting* or *shittin' me* is vulgar and in my book not really profanity
like *mother effin'*, etc. I think you get my point. When and if you finally
leave and get emancipated you will be working jobs and you must get in
the habit of speaking the queen's speech, not ghetto talk. The good thing
is that you have a whole year to get your act together."

"Thank you, honey, for your insightful information," returned Chester with a smile.

"Let us get back to profanity or *mother effin'*," continued Toni. "So, you
all know what it means and what might be the consequence for the first
infraction? You have paper and pencils, so please write down the consequence and then Mrs. T. will collect them."

Some of the girls wrote down their answers, while others wrote down
something and crossed it out and wrote another response, tore that up,
and just threw it in the trash can.

"Goddamn!" yelled DJ. "I broke my pencil! Oops, I think I just swore.
But I stopped before I said 'Goddamn fuckin shit' like when I am really
pissed off!"

"Thank you for helping us see the light," Chester replied mockingly,
"now, no more seeing the light!"

The slips were collected and Chester began to carefully examine them.
"Any repeats and I will can them in the trash can. Get it? Can them in the
trash can? Poetical if I do say so myself!"

Only DJ responded, "Can we please get on with this and can all the
stupid talk?"

Chester ignored DJ and went through the slips of paper and discarded
five repeats.

"Okay," he said reading one slip. "Here's one . . . first offense should
be a warning, second an apology, and third you write a one-page paper
as to why you should use other words instead of profanity or wolfing."

"Not bad," said Toni. "The person is suggesting ownership . . . which
is half the battle. Are there any other suggestions?"

Toni waited for a response but the girls remained silent, thinking.
Then she looked over at Chester as if to say, *Maybe they are finally taking
this seriously.*

Chester only responded with a nod of the head, like *Too early to get
happy.*

"Okay," she added. "Now, let's have a show of hands. Who supports this consequence?"

About three-fourths of the girls raised their hands and about 90 percent of the staff.

Chester read another slip. "Well, this one says 'Wash their mouth out with Coca Cola.'"

"Well," shouted DJ, "What if you don't like Coca Cola? That would be a bad consequence."

Chester ignored DJ and read a few others and came to one slip. After reading it, he nodded his head and read: "First offense, an apology; second offense, counseling and a two-page paper why profanity is not a good way to express yourself; the third offense, counseling and write a three-page paper about why people swear and possibly Front Street?"

Anthony looked over at Jewels, who just stared silently at the floor.

"Okay," said Chester, becoming animated with his hands. "Now, raise your hands if you agree to the last two suggestions."

The girls all raised their hands.

"Now raise your hands if you like the first one."

About three-fourths of the girls raised their hands and about half of the staff raised their hands.

"Okay, now raise your hands if you like the second!"

About one-third of the girls liked the second example and almost 100 percent of staff.

"I suggest an addendum to the second suggestion," said Michael, a tall, neatly dressed black man and the girls' counselor. "Why not include a two-page paper as part of an English assignment to support the GED pretests?"

The girls all liked his suggestion, as well as the staff.

"Remember," reminded Toni, "if you abstain, then you can't complain if you disagree with the consequence when you show up at the DC meeting."

The creation of the first rule and consequence lasted about thirty minutes and then Chester suggested a bathroom break.

The girls left for their bathroom break, which evolved into a cigarette and music break on the front porch until Chester threatened to eliminate all smoking and music privileges during the constitutional convention.

The next offense was wolfing or calling someone out of her given name. Wolfing was more difficult than swearing because the girls argued that wolfing is when you get really emotional and sometimes you can't stop yourself.

After about a half hour of debate, the girls and staff came up with the following: "First offense: warning and counseling; second offense, counseling and a written paper why wolfing is not an effective way to express your feelings; third offense, counseling, a two-page paper, and loss of a weekend outing; fourth offense, counseling, three-page paper, and possibly Front Street and possible expulsion!"

The girls adjourned for lunch and one hour later, it was back to the drawing board for more rules and consequences.

Now that the girls had a better understanding of how the constitutional convention worked, they also developed the ability for discourse and compromise, particularly with weekend curfew issues.

Most of the girls wanted 11:00 p.m. on Saturday nights with a twenty-minute grace period before being late.

Chester and Toni wanted 9:30 p.m. It took about an hour to hammer out the curfew deadline, which resulted in 10:30 p.m. and a fifteen-minute grace period.

JEWELS ODOM COMMENTARY #17

Chester and Ronnie think they are being slick about how they try to sell us on rules, consequences, and curfews. Whenever they suggest a rule and a consequence for curfews, it is always higher or lower than what we want. For example, with weekend curfews, they said 9:30 p.m., which blew us out of our seats! Really? By the time we dress or whatever we have to do to get ready to go out, it's already 8:30 p.m.! This means we have only an hour to be out and then there are all these places that are off limits, which only takes more time! By the time we figure out where we want to go, it's time to be back home.

What they should have known was that we are pros when it comes to bartering and compromising because that is how we survived on the streets. Chester and Toni thought they were teaching us how to compromise when we were really teaching them as well. If they went low, or wanted us to return back to school at 9:30 p.m., we went high and said 11:30 p.m., which blew them out of their seats as well! But after a great deal of going back and forth, we got them to agree to a 10:30 p.m. curfew.

Toni had the girls deposit their names into a bowl for the selection of the first two students to serve on the DC committee. Naturally, there were different degrees of anticipation and motives as to who the first two committee members would be.

"If I am selected," announced DJ, deliberately flashing a wide smile so her front gold tooth could sparkle, "I will try not to be too hard on you guys, and don't expect me to take any bribes of food either."

"Well," said Jewels. "We need to take the DC committee seriously. Do I need to remind you again? If this school fails than we all fail and it is back to the hall or CYA."

"Once again Jewels is running her mouth, thinking she is in charge when the ones in charge are Toni and Chester," said Patricia curtly.

"Thank you, DJ, Jewels, and Patricia for your excellent input," Toni said, selecting two names from the bowl, causing anxious looks from the students.

"Drum roll please," stated Toni, banging on a desk. "And . . . the two students to serve on DC for the month of October are Jewels and Patricia!"

Jewels glanced over at Anthony and then at Toni and only nodded her head.

"Okay," said Toni, "we will see you two in a week, Friday at 3 p.m., upstairs in Chester's office, for DC. Again, never be late because you will get written up, and as you know, too many write-ups will move you to Front Street and expulsion from the program. Any questions?"

JEWELS ODOM COMMENTARY #18

Serving on the DC is a big deal not only because it is a month-long assignment but what's really important is it forces us to see our world according to rules and consequences and not simply to side with each other. Again, remember we are street smart, our lives were based on survival, or you scratch my back and I will scratch yours and so forth.

Toni always reminds us that there will not be any gray areas about interpretation of the rules and consequences, only what was all agreed on by staff and students. Still, we all know she is preparing us that rule-breakers will argue the infraction, especially if the rule-breaker is close to Front Street, which could mean sending us back to juvie. Bottom line—when you serve on DC, your conscience will be challenged big time by your relationships with other students and staying in the program, like gray areas would mean students could "play the dozens," which was a phrase that Chester uses for when you try to talk yourself out of a rule violation or whatever. And it doesn't help when DJ whispers to Angel, "I know I can beat this system. Just watch me play my Perry Mason Act!"

SEVEN

Go Easy on DJ?

Anthony was standing in front of the class with the new GED teacher, Jamie Douglas, a petite blonde in her early thirties. She taught math at a local middle school and was teaching math part time at the Queen Street School's program for eleven- to sixteen-year-olds. The $64,000-dollar question circulating the school was, How did Anthony convince tightwad Chester to get Jamie to help him teach the GED to the older girls at the Clark Academy? It had become a major topic of discussion by staff and students.

"Either he got something on Chester," commented Mrs. T., "or Chester must have won the lottery."

"No way would Mr. Tightwad increase her hours to teach here, which means more money, and no way would he ever do that," explained Patricia, shaking her head vigorously.

"Anthony must have taken a pay cut for sure," offered Jewels.

"Anthony offered him this hot woman," suggested Kim. "That's all. The old man's trying to hold on to his you know what?"

Anthony would take care of all administrative work, such as IEPs, testing, backing up Jamie with her GED teaching, as well as oversee an afternoon program that included field trips, community volunteer jobs, and so on.

"Today we will pass out your GED books," announced Anthony. "And of course they are for you to keep. We will begin on page 2, 'Preparation Philosophy' or 'Steps to Success'; then discuss the actual General Education Development tests beginning with section 1, "Reasoning through English," which has three sections. The first section is thirty-five minutes long. Section 2 is forty-five minutes and section 3 is sixty minutes in duration. There are two math sections, and both are 115 minutes; plus science for one ninety-minute period and social studies for seventy minutes. The exact total minutes will be seven hours and thirty minutes. We will space out your studies over the next ten months until June."

"So," said Kim, interrupting Anthony, "like you're saying since we got the time . . . then there is no need to whine?"

"That's so lame!" yelled Angel. "It's still a test and if we don't pass it's *hasta la vista*, baby!"

"We will follow this process for the next two to three weeks," said Anthony, ignoring Angel. "We will work mornings and then play in the afternoon with field trips and so forth. I want you girls to enjoy the process until we feel you are ready to take the pretests."

"And the best part," interrupted Jamie, "is if you pass one section, you don't ever have to take it a second time!"

The girls only squirmed with discomfort a bit, but with very skeptical looks on their faces.

However, the mood changed when Mrs. T. appeared from a side door carrying a box of GED pretests into the classroom. "Sorry," she said, "but Mr. Chester wants you all to begin taking the GED pretests today."

Anthony looked over at Jamie with a concerned expression. The girls didn't need any more failures in their lives. His fear was that if some of the girls truly did bomb the pretests without preparation, they might run back to the streets and end up in juvie again.

Each girl had a different take on Mrs. T.'s announcement, which was first voiced by Patricia: "Let me get this straight! Mr. Know-It-All Chester really thinks we are really ready to take the stupid GED thing today? Hello! Like we haven't even practiced sitting down for longer than fifteen minutes. Now, we're supposed to sit for forty-five minutes? Anyhow, DJ will get blisters on her you-know-what because of gravity and all!"

"See, you already know science," responded Mrs. T. "Now, girl, sit down and keep it zipped." She mimed zipping her lips closed.

"Girl," said DJ with a look of chagrin. "Don't talk about me like I have a weight problem. You're all jealous because black men like big women, and you can take that to your next aerobics class!"

"Well, if this is what Chester really wants, then this is what Chester gets," interrupted Anthony, attempting to change the energy and conversation. "We have less than ten months before the real test at the JC. Today you can take the math pretest and work for only thirty-five minutes, stop, and take a break. We can stretch this out over as long as it takes to finish the pretests."

"Kind of like having dessert?" asked DJ.

JEWELS ODOM COMMENTARY #19

Passing the GED is not going to be a cake walk for even the most motivated and intelligent of students! And to say that we are motivated and have average academics skills would be speaking an untruth! I know all about the GED because that's what I had done the previous three months while in juvie. I found a "How to Pass the GED" book and spent most of my free time studying. I never told Chester or Toni because I was afraid they would make me take the test right off. If I passed I would be emancipated and county social services would help me find a job and hopefully a place to live. The million-dollar question that was always hangin' over our heads was . . . what kind of job? One that only paid minimum wage? Then where would I be living?

Again, passing the GED is not going to be a cake walk. For us students to pass the GED would be asking a lot, and our failure could place us back on the streets whoring, sellin' drugs, or joining some gang. Hello! What did they expect would happen if us girls failed? So now Chester had screwed up royally because he didn't have the balls to meet with Toni, Jamie, and of course us. Instead, he sends Mrs. T to do his dirty work to play Man on the Floor games, which is what we have been dealing with our entire lives. Again, from my father's abandonment, my mother's OD, the drug dealers, pimps, gangs, to even social services, who made all our decisions like where we lived and what school we attended. Finally, let's not forget the hall and the Louises of the world, the judge, PO's (often males), and then we got Chester doing his screw-you thing.

The same afternoon, after trying to recover from the shock of administering the GED pretests, Anthony sat alone at his desk in the Clark School office. Sitting across from Anthony was Jewels, staring intensely at the floor and refusing to make eye contact. Anytime a student ended up in the second-floor office, their initial reaction was always fear, or *What did I do to get sent back to the hall?* That matched the expression on Jewels's face.

Anthony stood up and began to pace back and forth with a worried expression.

"Okay," she said defensively. "I know I haven't done nothing wrong. I have followed every rule. I haven't smoked weed yet, but I would have liked to, so what's the problem, Mr. Teacher Man on the Floor?"

"I called you up to the school office because I have good news and some bad news for you. Do you want the good news or the bad news first?"

Jewels shook her head and said, "Just give me the news, man! Stop playing with my mind. This isn't *Let's Make a Deal!*"

Anthony flashed a questioning look at her and said, "Well, the good news is you passed the math and English pretests with flying colors. The bad news . . . about half the students didn't get close, and the other half are not far behind the first half."

"Is that what you called me up here for?" questioned Jewels. "What planet are you from? What did you expect? Hello?"

"You were in the hall for the past three months, and I assume they offered classes in passing the GED."

Jewels laughed and replied angrily, "I am not an idiot! On the unit, after school and most nights, there is really nothing to do. I figured I would not go back to regular school so I found a *How to Pass the GED* test book on the unit. I have been studying for almost three months."

"You can take the GED at the JC this week," explained Anthony. "You can pass it and move on to greener pastures."

"That's a great idea," said Jewels in disbelief. "Like if I pass it I'll get a penthouse in the freakin' city and a job earning a hundred grand a year. Man, get a clue! You people don't get it. I have no sugar daddy or mommy dearest to go back to. I have no place to go! For now, this is as good as it gets."

She got up and looked out the window and continued, "After this happy acres school, I'm on my own! Like I'm eeeeeemancipated to where and what? This is like when they freed the slaves, except now I got a high school diploma, and I'm working for $10.00 an hour doing fast food. I thought you were smarter than Chester. Bottom line: If I pass the GED, I'll end up back on the streets, which could mean I might end up usin' and abusing . . . doin' my n****r act. No way! I'm stayin' and gettin' clean for the next ten months. Nice bed, three meals a day, money to do laundry, and they even started a savings account for me. Hello!"

"No way, Mr. Teacher Man on the Floor. I'm staying, and if you tell my PO or Chester that I passed the GED pretests, I will flunk the real test on purpose and come back here and make your life miserable. Let's play *Let's Make a Deal*. Don't tell, and I will help you get these girls to pass the GED. It's a no-brainer. You need me, the girls need me, and I need you. See? Everyone wins."

"So, why help these girls?" asked Anthony. "I thought it was everyone for themselves, you know, the survival game? This hasn't been some love fest and I don't expect it to get any better."

"Why should I hate them when they're the same as me? No, what I do hate is what we stand for: mistakes by some man's penis that got lost in my mother's vagina! That's all it is. Losers who left us and our mothers who screwed them, but the real people we really hate are the white honkie johns who came around looking for tail . . . our mothers for a little fun. I can still hear the honking sound of those cars, then us kids would come running for our mamas and yell, 'The honkie man is here, Mama!' And our mamas would leave us alone again. It's something we all know and hate. Anything else, honkie man? They took me away before I knew what was happening, but it goes on all the time."

Anthony stared silently at the floor.

"Just do not be the honkie man and screw up my life again—that's all I ask," Jewels explained. "Seriously, do you freakin' understand?"

Anthony nodded his head and said, "Okay . . . deal." They shook hands and Jewels walked away slowly, shaking her head.

JEWELS ODOM COMMENTARY #20

I am not sure if I'm cutting my throat by agreeing to help Anthony. First of all, the girls still don't trust me because I refuse to get caught up in their ghetto head or how they dress, the tats, their homeboys, the sexual acting-out thing, or just the whole street scene they can't give up. If they find out that I am like an undercover snitch to help Anthony, it could really screw up my chances of staying the ten months, getting my GED, and so forth. Although I am still on the fence about helping him, I sure as hell do not want to pass the test early and become emancipated. I just need time to get my head and body together before I get back on my own!

EIGHT

Man on the Floor!

The term *Man on the Floor* was not a new term to Anthony because he had worked residential treatment, aka the psyche unit, at a county hospital in southern California for three years. He was fully aware of the possible pitfalls that confronted males when they worked residential treatment centers for women.

The County Hospital Psyche Unit was divided between sixteen men on one side and sixteen women on the other. The term *man on the floor* was always required when you conducted bed checks or simply supervised as a man on the women's side of the psyche unit. However, late-night bed checks or the eleven-to-seven graveyard shift was always the most problematic, which was why the "man on the floor" announcement was always required to avoid potential conflicts with the women, either physical or sexual accusations, regardless that most of the patients were medicated.

Interestingly, there was not much discussion at Anthony's hiring as to how to deal with sexually active street girls. The only time anyone mentioned the Man on the Floor cliché was on the day of Anthony's interview when Mrs. T. explained, "You always want to yell 'man on the floor' for fear of being in a compromising situation." It was for this reason that Anthony rarely if ever ventured upstairs to the school office nearest the girls' bedrooms, unless he was going to meet with Chester or Toni. If he did, however, it was usually after school when the girls were out and about in the hood, since freedom always took precedent over hanging out in their rooms, for obvious reasons.

On this particular afternoon, Anthony ventured upstairs to his office to go through a few potential new student files. The upstairs was its usual quiet atmosphere, although he still announced loudly, "Man on the floor!" Nevertheless, when he opened the office door, he found Sonya, a black seventeen-year-old girl, alone on a couch dressed only in panties and bra with a look on her face that asked for more than she should have been asking for.

Anthony was shocked, but more disappointed with Sonya because it would probably mean she would be expelled and sent back to juvie, thus ending her opportunity to get a high school diploma and her crimes expunged. Where she would end up in life was anyone's guess.

Anthony calmly stated, "I think you need to get dressed and we will have to deal with you later when Chester and Toni return from the Queen Street School."

Sonya had a look of surprise and said, "What is your problem? Can't you get it up, old man?"

When Anthony was about to leave the office, she said angrily, "It's your fucking loss!"

When Toni and Chester returned, Anthony explained to them what had happened. Chester only shook his head in disappointment, "I need to call her social worker and PO and all of us will need to meet this afternoon before I send her back to the hall. In all likelihood, she will stay at the hall until she meets with the judge to determine another placement. Of course," he continued, "you will need to fill out the paperwork describing the entire incident in case she gets into a 'he said, she said' thing. I mean, considering her background, but you never know—these things can get messy." Chester paused. "Just be careful what you say. I mean, did you announce, 'Man on the floor'?"

Anthony looked at Chester. "What do you think?"

"Sorry, but I always have to ask. It's part of my job."

For the next few days, all the discussion about Anthony and Sonya was hushed, and a week later the incident was forgotten since the girls had already moved on. Sonya was moved to a residential treatment facility for evaluation and that was last anyone heard from her.

JEWELS ODOM COMMENTARY #21

We never really know what it's like to be in Anthony's head when it comes to us girls. I mean, we are all grown women with these great bodies who have been around the block when it comes to our sexuality. And then we are always walking around in our bathrobes or PJs and dancing seductively to music. We sometimes catch him looking at us, but it never comes across as sexual. Although there was one time when Kim came up to his desk for help. She was wearing this not-so-conservative blouse. She bent down in front of him and you couldn't miss what her intentions were. While Anthony was explaining to her a certain math problem, his eyes wandered, and then he stopped for a moment and lost his train of thought. Then DJ yelled out, "Easy boy, we know it's getting hard! I mean, the teaching!"

Anthony got all embarrassed and annoyed. He didn't say a word and just continued with his sentence about how to do the math problem. We all moved on, sort of feeling sorry for him, realizing we were sexually harassing him in the reverse. Again, I think it was difficult for him, hard, but not in what DJ was insinuating, if you get my drift!

NINE

She Forgot Her Pot?

Anthony enrolled the Clark Academy girls in a University of California pottery class to lessen the stress of passing the GED test, as well for the experience of the positive energy of a college campus. The chance to rub elbows with multiracial and multicultural male and female students as well as having the experience of different physical characteristics of the UC student body, such as short hair, long hair, braided hair, straight hair, and females dressed in a variety of clothing instead of the tight black slacks, low-fitting halter tops, the black spiked heels, or the uniforms of street walkers would be revelatory for the girls.

Some of the Clark Academy girls were working at various tables kneading clay, and others were being supervised by pottery studio assistants as to how to work the clay and keep it wet.

Kim and Angel worked at a table, eliminating air holes out of the clay by cutting the clay on wires and then throwing the clay back on a cement surface while repeating the same exercise over and over again. Only Kim and Jewels worked at the potter's wheel.

Jewels tried to throw a pot, but the pot immediately collapsed. She became embarrassed and looked around to see if anyone saw her numerous failures, yet she persevered and started over until another failure. Finally, a male student named Johnathan Simon, who was working at a wheel next to her, leaned over and offered to help her.

Johnathan, age twenty, had an all-American-boy look. He was tall, blonde, personable, looking like someone you might see as a model in an *Orvis* magazine.

"Looks like you need a little help?" he asked Jewels.

Jewels responded shyly, "Errrr, no, well . . . maybe?"

"It's how you shape the clay with your hands," he explained, "a little like holding an egg firmly, but not too firmly, and then let the wheel work for you."

Jewels tried to throw another pot, but in seconds, it failed again.

"Do you mind?" asked Johnathan. "Let me help you."

Johnathan took Jewels's hands and gently held them against the clay.

"Great," he said. "Now apply the right amount of pressure. The clay will form into a perfect symmetrical vase."

When Johnathan let go of Jewels's hands, the vase fell apart.

"I'm sorry," she said, embarrassed. "It's my fault. I'm such a klutz! I will never get this right!"

Johnathan held out his muddy hand to Jewels to formally introduce himself, until he realized he needed to clean his hands first.

"Sorry," he said, reaching for a rag. He wiped his hands and then passed the rag to Jewels, who wiped her hands clean.

"Let's try this again," he said, reaching out to shake Jewels hand. "My name is Johnathan Simon and . . . ?"

"Oh!" she said, embarrassed, "my brain went dead. Sorry, my name is Jewels . . . Jewels Odom." Then they shook hands.

"And Miss Odom," Johnathan returned, "what school are you in?"

Jewels hesitated and responded confused, "Ahhh! Yes! I do go to a school!"

"Good," pursued Johnathan. "Now what school? English? Education? You got the look of an English major. I am a terrible writer," he continued, "even though my father teaches here in the English Department."

"No! Yes!" she said nervously. "Education! I like education."

"Elementary or secondary?" he probed.

Jewels responded, "Can I choose? Ooops," she said, moving quickly to the door, "I think I see my classmates leaving." She waved back at Johnathan. "Nice to meet you!"

"Hey!" hollered Johnathan confused. "It doesn't matter! What about your bowl?"

Jewels raced out of the pottery studio and ducked around a corner.

Johnathan ran to the front door to catch her, but Jewels had quickly disappeared among the hundreds of students on the quad. Johnathan returned to the pottery studio and found the pottery instructor.

"Do you know the name of the school those new girls attend?" he asked. "One girl left her pot . . . I mean her bowl and I want to get it to her."

"I believe," said the teacher, thinking, "the Clark Academy."

"Great!" shouted Johnathan. "Thank you . . . thank you!"

JEWELS ODOM COMMENTARY #22

Having suggested the pottery class to Anthony, I remember now what the pottery teacher at the hall had stated. Our teacher had said that the clay was grounding and any rage or anger would always leave my body each time I worked the clay. Also, she said that holding and squeezing the clay gave us the feeling of control, which was something we had never really had in our past lives. Finally, seeing a bowl or cup come to completion gave me a sense of satisfaction, something we needed on an everyday basis to get through the juvenile hall experience. Fortunately, Anthony almost always follows through with my suggestions. The pottery class at UC Berkeley is turning out to be one of my best suggestions.

TEN

She Took off the Band-Aids!

For Anthony and Jamie's GED class, the girls were actually on time, sitting at their desks with rolled-up butcher paper. Anthony announced they would write their life scripts on five- by three-foot butcher paper with magic markers. At first, they used the rolled-up butcher paper to sword fight; others used them as musical instruments to blow air through them, while still others pretended to use them as telescopes. Finally, when the girls moved on from the novelty of the rolled-up butcher paper, Anthony announced, "This writing exercise is to help you with the GED English test, but also to aid in developing self-awareness. Jamie could not be here because she has a few loose IEP ends at the Queen Street school, so I will do the class today."

"I can't write about myself because . . . well, errrrrr," stuttered Tina, "I'm trying to forget stuff. I do not need to go over when my daddy got shot."

"She's right," said DJ, never missing a chance to get out of doing schoolwork. "I don't want to write about some of my homeboys who are in jail or got shot too."

After a measurable degree of persuading why writing about themselves could lay the foundation for other writing lessons, they all agreed to try.

Writing about their earliest memories to the present could help the girls open up and deal with their pasts, which were filled with many painful memories inflicted by males and females from all walks of life.

After about an hour of writing, Anthony gave the girls a ten-minute break before they would return to class. The hard part was getting one of the girls to take the plunge and volunteer to read her life script to the class.

Anthony waited in silence until finally Jewels stood up and proceeded to walk to the front of the classroom.

Jewels stared intensely at Anthony and said, "Okay, okay! I will go first!"

She looked at Anthony again and mouthed the words, *Remember, only till June.*

"Jewels agreed to go first," declared Anthony, trying to hold back his obvious excitement as well as appreciation that Jewels was following through on their agreement to help move the girls away from their deep mistrust and suspicion that constantly appeared whenever any man, even Anthony, asked them to open up emotionally and personally.

Jewels began to read slowly from her paper.

"All you have to know is that I was born in Oakland, California. My smuck bio-father, who I never met, was named Johnny-the-loser. My user druggie mother's name was supposed to be Mimi. They said I had lived with her for my first year of life, which always made me feel good even though I was told that I was the result of a one-night-stand with Johnny, the loser. My user mother said that Johnny-the-loser ended up in prison for sellin' drugs and when he got out he was shot dead when a drug deal went south. My user junkie mother OD'd on some bad heroin a few years ago . . . so they told me."

"You can stop if you want and have someone else read their script," interrupted Anthony, attempting to give Jewels a reprieve, but she shook her head and continued to read on.

"The good news was that when I was about a year old, I was taken from my mother and put in a foster home. She got me back when I was about three and that lasted only a few months until they found me wandering on the streets alone one night. Yeah! That was the last time I ever lived with my loser druggie mother. Actually, I was placed in so many different foster homes, I could fill up this entire page. By the time I was ten years old, I got placed in a school for crazies because I hated anything that moved so they gave me this important title, S.E.D., or seriously emotionally disturbed."

She turned to Anthony, "Like you wouldn't be pissed off if you had experienced my childhood? Big words that don't say anything about my loser daddy and a druggie, hoe mother and a one-night-stand and a bottle of Ripple or whatever. The worse part about the school was how they played with my mind, like when they brought me to adoption fairs. That was real fun. It was like getting a tattoo on my brain."

"My social worker, a tall black woman named Mrs. Peterson, came into my room one day with this new dress and said, 'We're going to an adoption fair. Jewels, I got you this dress to wear at the adoption fair tomorrow. After we do your hair, you will be the most beautiful child at the fair. Then every couple will want to adopt you!'

"Like I really wanted to have to sit in a chair while all these people walked by me and looked at me like they're buying a piece of fruit. The next day my social worker tried to fix my hair, which you can guess was, like, real nappy!"

Jewels stopped and took a few deep breaths, asking, "Anyone got any questions?"

"Yea," asked DJ. "what did she use on your hair?"

Jewels flashed DJ a pissed-off look, "What the hell are you asking me that question for when all I want to do is forget that time of my life?"

"The look she was giving all of us is to please let her get through this bullshit reading," interrupted Tina. "So let the poor girl finish!"

"Sorry," apologized DJ, "but don't stop. I want to find out more about the stupid adoption fair and you feeling like a piece of shit."

"We get to this auditorium with all these other kids," continued Jewels. "We sat behind a table and waited for the people to check me out. There were mostly younger kids up for sale . . . I mean adoption. Like really young kids and I got the feeling that there was no way in hell that they would want to adopt a black nine-year-old loser kid. So, there are all these kids . . . black, white, brown, green . . . only joking . . . all sitting behind tables while adults walked around, looking at the different kids, again like they were shopping for some new car or clothes. Not only did I feel like shit, but I had to put on this fake smile when they passed. Inside I felt like dying, and the worse part was no one ever stopped to even ask my fucking name!"

Jewels was about to become emotional when Patricia piped up and said, "Screw them! You didn't need no loser parents who couldn't have their own loser kids!"

"Okay, let me go on," said Jewels, waiting for Patricia to cool down. "It was late afternoon and me and my social worker and a few other older loser kids were the only ones left in the large auditorium. We finally left and when I got into the social worker's car, I started crying. I told her I knew I would never have a family and that the people didn't want an ugly black kid! The social worker agreed and said that we would never go to one of those fairs again."

Jewels stopped reading from the paper and asked if anyone had any questions, but the girls all remained quiet.

"Okay," said Jewels. "And guess what? I was stupid enough to let them take me to two more adoption fairs, and guess what? I never got adopted, and guess what? I couldn't do it anymore so I ran away again and again. And guess what? They said I was crazy and put me in another home for kids, but it was really an institution for whackos. Funny, but I guess I'm still in an institution, only they call it the Clark Academy!"

Jewels got up quietly and tore up her life script into little pieces and was about to walk out of the room when she stopped and turned to Anthony and the rest of the students and said, "Every little piece of my paper you all see on the floor is a piece of me." Then she mumbled under her breath, "I did my part, now help us pass the GED. That's all we ask."

JEWELS ODOM COMMENTARY #23

Reading my life script was a killer! Anytime you have to deal with your past is difficult, but something very strange happened to me when I wrote it all down and then shared it with the rest of the world. I got a different feeling, a kind of release, although it brought out a great deal of anger when I read it out loud to the girls who had also gone through some of the same things. I mean it was like I had taken off the Band-Aid and felt the cut had finally healed!

ELEVEN
When Art Therapy Becomes Talk Therapy

Anthony lived with his girlfriend Madison, an art therapist, in the Berkeley Beverly Hills, as they called it. He had hoped he could enlist her to do art therapy sessions with the girls, but she was hesitant because of the sensitivity of art therapy with such troubled youth.

"Trust is a crucial issue," she explained to him, "particularly with an outsider like myself who must deal with clients and their most intimate emotions and memories. I would want to wait until the girls learn to trust you before I would expect them to trust me."

Once Anthony had worked at the school for a few months, Madison consented to conduct a series of classes with the girls, which she called "tapping into the creative process."

Madison met with Toni to discuss her art therapy sessions.

"My concerns involve the girls' traumatic pasts, which could trigger angry responses," explained Madison. "Are you prepared for that?"

"We can handle it," said Toni confidently. "Obviously, it would be great for the girls to get their anger out, which could facilitate more positive feelings about their past traumas."

Again, Madison reiterated, "I would need to establish relationships with the girls before I did any sessions, mainly talking about what they would expect if and when I commit to the sessions."

A few weeks later, Madison appeared for the girls' first art therapy session. The girls were all giggly meeting Anthony's girlfriend for the first time and all sorts of questions ensued.

"Does he cook?"

"Is he neat or sloppy?

"How did you meet?"

"Where did you go on your first date?"

"Is our guy going to get married?"

"How many dates did you have until you did it?"

Finally, Madison said seriously, "No more questions. It's time we discuss art therapy and the method I like to call tapping into the creative process. The entire purpose of my art therapy class is to open up the creative process as you also address your deepest emotions," she explained to the five girls who were then selected alphabetically for the first class.

She had Juan, the school's janitor, place some long tables on the backyard lawn. Next, she set out ten sheets of newspaper and about eight bottles of different tempura paints and brushes for each student.

She would see five girls at a time for thirty minutes of getting to know them, thirty minutes of painting, and another thirty minutes for discussion.

Once more she said, "When you open up the creative process, you also free up your emotions. In other words, your pasts will play a great deal in the process, or again your deepest emotions. Art therapy sessions may seem harmless, but they can also be very powerful, so just let your emotions come up at will. If you feel overwhelmed, just take short, slow breaths, and that should calm you."

For the first part of the class, she asked the girls to speak about their pasts. Although she expected some resistance, the girls all seemed comfortable describing how they ended up in the juvenile correctional system. Only when they came to the death of a loved one did they stop and refuse to speak about such incidents.

Finally, after all five girls finished speaking about their pasts, they moved to their respective tables.

"I must repeat," she explained seriously," the purpose is for you to take only two minutes to cover the entire newspaper in whatever colors you choose. This is a non-thinking exercise so use as many colors as you want. When I say time's up, you will place the finished paper on the grass and take another sheet of paper and follow the same procedure until you have completed ten sheets. Again, I want you to take short, effortless breaths if you are feeling too emotional, and there will be no talking or engagement with other students. If I see you speaking or engaging with other girls, I will ask you to leave.

"Any questions? Let's begin."

Toni sat off to the side, observing the class. It was her hope that as clinical director, she would be able to follow the same procedures as Madison and continue with the non-thinking painting exercises with the girls.

After twenty minutes, the girls were able to complete ten drawings. At first, some of the girls complained that they had not finished some of their paintings in only two minutes, but Madison explained that she was not interested in the process of finishing each painting, but only getting your emotions out onto the paper.

When they were through, Madison and the five girls walked around each table to explain what they saw in the drawings of each participant. At first harmless appraisals appeared until they got to about the fourth or fifth drawing of each girl and harmless interpretations turned to anger and tears.

"I see lots of anger in this drawing of Kim's," said Jewels in a sympathetic voice. "Look at the black and then she goes to white and then over here back to black."

Kim was speechless and only nodded her head and then broke down in tears. "Well, this is my father, who was killed in a bad drug deal. I'm sorry, but that is all I can say."

Kim pulled back, dropped her head, and continued to sob. Jewels came over and gave her a hug, and then Angel followed with another hug.

Madison suggested that Kim try to do some deep breathing to deal with her emotions.

"I told you this is a very powerful exercise and not to be taken lightly. After you complete several sessions, you should begin to feel some healing . . . like a bad dream finally coming out that you have held inside you for so long."

Madison stayed for another hour, going over the different paintings with the girls.

She reminded the girls that they might experience powerful dreams that night and to do some stretching exercises, yoga, or deep breathing if their feelings became so intense that they needed to speak with Toni.

That night Anthony received a call from Mary, the 11 p.m. to 7 a.m. night counselor, who explained, "Some of the girls couldn't sleep and Kim and Bonita nearly had a fight."

JEWELS ODOM COMMENTARY #24

This had to be the most intense therapy sessions I have ever experienced! All the bullshit talk-therapy sessions were nothing compared to what we all experienced this day. Madison came for one more session to work with us and then Toni would pick-up the class and follow the same lessons as Madison. Toni would touch base with Madison to discuss the classes. Bottom line—although there were always lots of tears and emotions, we knew it was good because no one was ever sick or missed a class!

TWELVE

Mr. Buddha Man on the Floor?

Jewels was sitting on the steps of the old mansion-turned-academy, looking very discouraged and depressed. A Buddhist monk named Brother Chi was making his daily trip to his Buddhist center on the sidewalk in front of the Clark Academy. He was dressed in his traditional orange robe and leather sandals, head shaved bare. Though he was about thirty-five years of age, he had the face of a twenty-five-year-old. Jewels gave him a half-hearted smile and returned to her anguish about the school, the Clark Academy girls, and the pressure of the GED test.

In the past, Brother Chi had seen Jewels sitting in the same location and had always given her a friendly wave with a smile and Jewels had always reciprocated with a friendly wave back. However, on this day Jewels didn't return his wave. Sensing something was wrong with Jewels, he walked up to where she was sitting.

In his broken English, he said, "I'm Brother Chi. This your school? Each day, on my way to temple, I see you and your students. Today you didn't wave back to me. Why so sad?"

Jewels flashed an embarrassed look at him and then pulled back and said defensively, "My name is Jewels, and yeah, I am a student here and yeah, I am worried about stuff. What's it to you?"

"Maybe I help you?"

"Oh yeah," exclaimed Jewels, "maybe you not help me! Maybe I do not need any chants to learn how to get DJ from eating Big Macs. Like you really, really think you can help me?! My pimp, Latrell, would have really liked you too. We got all this stuff in common, right?"

"I don't know what you mean," he questioned." Only, I know you go to school and maybe it is hard for you?"

"You want more truth?" she said sarcastically. "We have not been in real school in years and some of these students can barely read and write. You want truth? The truth is how are we goin' to pass the GED test and get emancipated? Or, if we do not pass the test, we could end up in some residential program for crazies, back at juvie, or even worse, end up back on the streets, dead, or in jail; so, there's a lot of truth! Now, don't tell me truth sets you free. It is all bullshit!" Jewels looked down at the ground and then at Brother Chi and laughed heartily.

"This might be a good time for students for me," he said with a smile. "I used to be math teacher in China. Maybe I help you girls? Help you pass, what you say, GED?"

"Here we go again with your life and our lives which are like Piedmont and us in East Oakland. We will steal, lie, cheat, gang bang, steal drugs, prostitute, do whatever we need to survive. Go find some place and chant for us so we can pass the GED test!"

"I will talk to my supervisor and you talk to yours and we talk again."

JEWELS ODOM COMMENTARY #25

So here I am talking to some monk who is trying to convince me that he can help us pass the GED. Our lives are going in opposite directions and he is thinking that he can help us? I only say to myself, "Stay tuned, Mr. Buddha Man on the Floor, for a major disappointment."

A week later Brother Chi was sitting quietly on the floor, cross-legged, waiting for the girls to become quiet and focused. Previously, he had met with Anthony and Chester to talk about teaching math to the girls. Today Chester and Anthony sat off in a corner of the classroom, ready to observe Brother Chi and his demonstration lesson.

Chi spoke in his usual quiet, calm voice, which reflected a sense of sincere honesty.

Chester whispered to Anthony, "The million-dollar question will be, can he handle the natives as well as teach math? All this mumbo jumbo meditation stuff works over there in his world, but can he handle these girls? Or is he only blowing smoke . . . am I right, or am I right?"

"Jewels asked me to come and help you with your GED math lessons," Chi explained to the girls, who surprisingly sat quietly at their desks, staring at this very strange man dressed in a weird costume.

"Mr. Barkley and your good teacher, Mr. Anthony, agreed to let me speak to you about teaching math to help you pass GED." He stopped momentarily as if to give the girls a chance to digest the strangeness of the situation and then continued, "First, I am a good teacher, but only if you listen and to do what I say. If you do not listen, I cannot help you. I believe you all can pass GED math section, but first, you must learn to trust and not resist my teaching. Like standing in river . . . too deep and you resist river's currents . . . harder to stand up. Go with flow; become part of river. It takes you where it needs to go. I can be the river's current. Trust me and go with flow and you become better learners and pass hard test."

The girls flashed tense smiles, squirmed in their seats, and waited quietly for Brother Chi to continue, but just before Brother Chi began his lesson, Chester had to leave due to a phone call and mumbled, "Sorry, Brother Chi, they never leave you alone. County Office of Education. Nothing is free, and Anthony to be safe I want you there as well."

"Chester and Anthony always get out of stuff!" yelled DJ, breaking the silence of the girls.

"Cuz," he responded with a smile, "I is the bill payer. *Nǐ bù dǒng ma?* It means 'Do you understand?'"

Mr. Chi only smiled, but remained silent, almost to let the girls' true energy and spirits appear.

"Excuse me," continued DJ, "I got something really important to say. How come you guys never get to do all the fun things in life like go to Clint's Barbecue, and you never have . . . you know what I mean, get hooshey!"

Bonita whacked DJ on her shoulder and asked, "Girl, what did you have for breakfast this morning? Because your horny hormones are kicking in. Please excuse DJ for being so horny hormonal!"

Mr. Chi remained silent.

"Well," said DJ, "it's true! No hooshey! No meat, no Clint's Barbecue, no Big Macs!"

DJ closed her eyes and pretended to meditate. "Never, never, never will I give up Clint's Barbecue ribs. Never, never will I give up mashed potatoes; never, never will I give up chicken, coleslaw. See, I got a lot to lose!"

"Are you finished?" asked Jewels, embarrassed by DJ's outburst.

DJ put her hands over her ears and sang, "I can't hear youuuuuuuu!"

"It is good you love food, but must need to learn to love numbers too," spoke Mr. Chi. "Numbers in your life all the time, especially when you learn math."

"How about these numbers, Mr. Buddhist Man? 36 . . . 24 . . . 36," said Kim, strutting around the classroom while sexually moving her hips.

"In your dreams," said Bonita, deliberately bouncing her breasts up and down. "I have seen those little fried eggs of yours. This is what you need." She stuck her chest in Patricia's face.

"With you it is more like melons!" Patricia yelled, pulling her face away.

Finally, Brother Chi spoke and said softly, "I want everyone to please push desks to the side. I have brought cushions for you to sit on, like I sit."

Mr. Chi passed out thirteen cushions and the girls followed his directions to sit on the cushions. Only DJ was reluctant at first until Jewels reminded her, "Chester and Anthony could be coming back soon and you don't want to piss Chester off, especially after speaking with the county about money."

Jewels's advice hit home and DJ plopped herself down on the cushion with a thud, regardless of the fact that she couldn't sit cross legged for obvious reasons. Instead, she just stuck her legs straight out, which, according to Mr. Chi, was "just fine."

"I would just like to teach you how to calm body before I do math lesson with you. A calm body means calm mind. To do well on test, you need calm mind . . . no pressure . . . no fear."

The girls remained surprisingly silent and waited patiently for Brother Chi to direct them to the next step.

"I want you to close eyes and slowly breathe in and out. I want breathing to be easy and effortless."

The girls began to slowly breathe in and out and almost immediately you could see their bodies begin to relax, become more vertical rather than hunched down with their breathing now less restricted, becoming slower and more rhythmic.

"Now I want you to listen to this sound," he directed. "I am going to make a sound while you continue to take effortless breaths."

Mr. Chi began to chant "Ommmmmmmmmmmmmm."

Some of the girls opened their eyes to the strange sound, but then closed their eyes and continued to breathe slowly for about five more minutes.

"Okay," he continued, "now slowly open your eyes, but try to stay with relaxed feeling you received from the breathing and listening to the sound of 'ommmmmmmmm.'"

When the girls opened their eyes, there was a sense of calmness reflected in their faces.

"So," asked Mr. Chi, "how you feel? Any difference?"

"I feel like I just had a nice quiet nap," said Jewels.

"I don't feel any stiffness in my neck," offered Patricia.

"I felt really relaxed and not pissed off at Kim for keeping me awake last night because she had a bad dream."

"We will take a break before I do a math lesson with you," he said. "Anyone who needs to use the bathroom, please go now."

About half the girls left but the others remained, sitting in their positions, waiting for the lesson to begin.

Minutes later, Chester and Anthony returned, appearing amused that the girls were all sitting on cushions while quietly listening to Mr. Chi. Chester didn't say a word, only respected the energy in the room.

JEWELS ODOM COMMENTARY #26

"It was really a trip to see our reaction to Mr. Chi's first math class. Not only did he calm us, but he changed our angry facial postures, which could, in past sessions, set another student off into their own anger. It felt like some drug had relaxed us."

Once the girls were all back and settled on their mats, Mr. Chi explained his math class to the girls.

"The GED math examples and the steps to do them are on sheets of paper that are placed throughout your school. You will take notebooks and go to papers and do pretest math problems on your own. I want you out of classroom. Make a change. Make it fun. Move around. Thirteen of you and twenty-six problems. There are two problems on every paper. I will pass out numbers where each of you will begin. Once start, then just follow the next number. When finished with problem, you move to next problem. You must love numbers too. Numbers are in your life all the time."

The girls continued to be silent and listened intently.

"Remember: repetition and success bring mastery. Please repeat whenever you get frustrated and always breathe in and out slowly. *Nǐ bù dǒng ma?*"

"Yeah," returned DJ, "we understand. See? We learn fast!"

The girls left for their treasure hunt to find their math problems.

"Repetition brings boredom and hunger," repeated DJ, walking out of the classroom. "Repetition brings boredom and hunger."

The girls seemed to like Mr. Chi's method. They departed from the classroom and scattered throughout the school, looking for the sheets of paper and where to start their math problem.

Bonita came to her first math example, located on the bathroom door. First, she looked at the steps to the example on the top of the sheet and then she worked on another example below without the steps on the bottom.

While she was doing the math example, she accidentally pushed the bathroom door too hard, and when it opened, she found DJ on the can.

"What the hell is going on?" DJ screamed. "I mean . . . I can't even take a dump without people barging in."

"Whoa mama!" screamed Bonita slamming the door shut. "Grossness with the mostness!"

Then Jewels appeared.

"Ahhhhh," warned Bonita to Jewels, "I like the guy's learning style, but next time he should leave the bathroom door off his lesson. I just saw DJ on the can and it was not a pretty sight."

Jewels flashed a confused look.

"Usually whenever I do math, it brings back old memories of failing in school. But doing the breathing before the lesson and then moving around and doing math this way made me feel different, especially if I can see how to do the problems first."

The girls returned to the classroom in about 30 minutes and sat down at their desks. Although the energy had changed from calmness, there was now a sense of excitement and a sense of confidence among some of the girls.

Chester and Anthony sat in chairs and observed the change in the girls' behavior. They didn't cap on each other, and they actually followed Mr. Chi's directions without any blowups.

On the way out, the girls thanked Mr. Chi, and even DJ said, "I hope you come back soon with another lesson and maybe even bring us lunch."

Mr. Chi smiled and looked at Chester. "Yes, very soon, but no lunch!"

JEWELS ODOM COMMENTARY #27

What was so strange to all of us was that although this is another Man on the Floor, he treated us not as young sexual creatures who men tried to control or get something from, but looked at us only as human beings who wit h true potential!

THIRTEEN

Playin' the Dozins

Anthony scheduled field trips every Friday and made a point to make them educational as well as fun, in order to support their academic program. The first field trip was to Channel 2, a popular TV station in the Bay Area. He felt that the girls had learned how to walk the talk on the streets to survive, so why not introduce them to a black professional male who talked and got paid for his work, which the girls said they had already done as hookers, drug dealers, and gang bangers?

On the way over to Channel 2, Anthony asked the girls to elaborate on how they walked the talk on the streets.

"Well," volunteered Kim. "You better be able to walk the talk on the streets because if you don't, the johns will win and you will lose, especially when your pimp wants his money." "The johns always try to talk you down and you always try to take a bigger cut by asking for more," volunteered Jewels. "The more you get, the larger the cut, except you don't tell the pimp—that's all."

"The same thing was when I was sellin' drugs," offered Bonita. "Druggies want their fun now and they will mostly go high to get high! The problem comes with the supplier, who will try to work you down, so you got to be smart and do your homework about what is sellin' on the streets and how much."

"I don't talk about my homeboys to nobody," said Angel. "That's if you don't want to get hurt."

Another reason for the trip was that they all wanted to see a black newsman "stud" named John Richardson.

99

When they arrived at the TV studio, the girls were first shown around the news room by a young, black female intern, who further reinforced Anthony's earlier speech: "It isn't the color of your skin that may get you in or keep you out, but your brains and perseverance."

Once they saw the studio, they settled into watching a live broadcast by their black stud.

During a commercial he waved to the girls, which was a big deal because, according to DJ, "I think he is goin' to call me up for an interview, because I am the best lookin' and you know I have other qualities that you all don't have."

"Oh yeah," said Kim, "like a commercial for Big Macs!"

Their black stud returned to the air and for the next 30 minutes, the girls actually remained quiet until it was time to leave. Finally, during another commercial, Mr. Richardson rushed over to shake all the girls' hands and pass on some advice.

"You can become anyone you want to be," he said, his professional voice not missing a beat. "It takes hard work and brains, which I know you all got. Maybe I will see one of you working as an intern here someday."

After the girls left, his words and presence left an impression that stayed with them for the journey back to school. However, again, it was DJ who had the last word: "You know he made eye contact with me the most. Maybe I will have a career in broadcasting, only they need to change the word *broad* in *broadcasting* to another word. It's like sexist!"

The girls remained quiet and didn't want to bust her bubble.

On the other hand, the field trip to the Albany racetrack was one of the most entertaining because they were allowed to walk around the stables feeding the horses, which they loved. However, what topped the feeding of the horses occurred with a group of young jockeys who came riding by, exercising their horses for an "afternoon breeze." When they viewed the girls, they immediately stuck their rear ends up high like roosters strutting around a henhouse. This gave the girls the excuse to hoot and holler, causing the jockeys to shake their booties, which created more yelling and hoots from the girls. Anthony thought it was ironic to see males using their bodies to sexually excite the girls. However, the girls just laughed when Jewels exclaimed, "Very cute, but don't you think we could give them a run for the money?"

The science boat trip on the bay was also one of the best because it was scientific and supported the science aspects of the GED. Anthony wanted to show the girls that science was not only from the book, but all around them and in their faces. Anthony chartered a 60-foot boat that catered to schools out on the bay. The boat dragged the bottom for a couple of hours to see what was down there. When they pulled the nets up, all sorts of local fish, crab, cans, bottles, and even a Safeway shopping cart appeared, which turned the girls off to no end.

"Well," said Kim, "it really pisses me off to see all the junk that people just throw into the bay. I mean, how would you like to be some crab or some poor fish and have to deal with people's crap? I know I will think twice about littering . . . and you can take that to the dump!"

Again, Anthony was looking for balance between GED testing and interesting excursions. Although the field trips moved the girls out of the school building, the field trips had serious ups and downs, like the day they drove out to the Pt. Reyes Lighthouse to see whales. Pt. Reyes Lighthouse was located at one of the most western regions of the U.S. continent and it was always a major attraction because it was still a working lighthouse. The only problem with the lighthouse visit was the 313 steps or equivalent 26 stories that led down to the lighthouse, which meant their return would require the students to walk back up the many steps.

DJ looked down at the lighthouse steps and said, "Whoa mama, this could be a major problem for DJ."

"Yeah," said Tina, "girl, you aren't seriously thinking of making the trip down to heaven, cuz coming back will be like going to hell! No way will you be able to get back. They will have to send helicopters or rescue people to carry you back."

DJ took offense and naturally said, "This will be a piece of cake!"

DJ started down the steps with the other girls and of course goin' down was like going to heaven or "a piece of cake." They made it down and walked around and saw the magnificent lighthouse that guided boats away from the rocky Pt. Reyes shore. They even heard the loud fog horn and although they didn't see any whales and only a few seals, overall it was educational, as well as good exercise. Though it took them only about fifteen minutes to get down, coming up was a serious challenge.

Fortunately, they could stop off on the way up at resting stations, which allowed them to take numerous breathers. However, the real problem was with DJ, who would walk fifteen steps and stop for a time, and then start up again. Finally, about halfway up, she gave up and simply sat down and refused to move. "You need to send in the coast guard or something, because I am definitely pooped in and out."

Angel and Jewels stayed with DJ while some of the girls returned with water. After about an hour, she finally made it back to the top.

"I thought I was going to have a 350-pound heart attack," she moaned.

"You even cheated on a heart attack," said Kim. "How about a 400-pound heart attack?"

"Anyway, next time I will look at the lighthouse from a distance like a big boat or whale—that's all."

JEWELS ODOM COMMENTARY #28

Anthony showed us a film called The Dirty Dozen *before we went on our first field trip. He didn't tell us very much about the movie, only that it was about a bunch of loser convicts who would get their freedom if they pulled off this big top-secret attack on some loser Nazis. The funny part about watching the movie was how we all capped on each other by connecting the different losers in the movie to us.*

Since there were many white guys and only one black guy, a hunk named Jim Brown, all us black girls said they were like him. Angel liked this old Hispanic singer-turned-actor called Trini Lopez. It was smart of Anthony to show us the film because when we were out in public, we realized that if one failed or screwed up, we all failed and screwed up. I think he got his point across with the movie because everyone actually was on her best behavior on the trip.

FOURTEEN

This Couch Really Sucks!

Chester motioned for Johnathan Simon to sit down on the "sucking couch." Johnathan was the UC student that Jewels met in the pottery class about a month ago.

"Please sit down, Johnathan. I don't bite . . . yet!" ordered Chester, sitting behind his cluttered desk. "Also, just to remind you, the couch has a tendency to be a little soft, so when you sit down, you will get the feeling that you are about a foot shorter than you really are."

When Johnathan sat down, the couch didn't disappoint and sucked Johnathan down the expected one foot. He tried to adjust himself or sit up, but the couch continued to suck him down like quicksand.

"I see you finally made it to the top of the food chain or Front Street," continued Chester. "Boy or man, you do not quit, do you? You must have called Miss Odom 100 times before she came to me. I like your perseverance, but not your brains. So, what can I do for you?"

"I . . . well," sputtered Johnathan, "I . . . well, I . . . I—"

"Spit it out, boy!"

"I—I wouldliketogetyourpermissiontotakeJewelsout . . . to my parents' dinner party," he stammered.

Chester carefully adjusted his posture, peered intensely at Johnathan, nodded his head, stood up and walked to a side bookcase, shook his head, moved back to his desk, sat down, and again peered closely at Johnathan.

"Boy, have you been smokin' those funny cigarettes again? Have you been reading the *Inquirer* newspaper and looking for some sensationalism? Are you tryin' to shock me? Take out Jewels? Are you talkin' about the same Jewels that you and I know?"

"Yes sir, the same . . . er, sir," said Johnathan in a hesitant voice.

"I read the book, but I'm not sure if I like the story," said Chester, getting up again from his chair. "Okay, let me articulate this better. Boy or man meets girl at pottery studio. Boy or man helps girl make a bowl or something like that. It is very romantic, except he don't know that he is out of his league, or like he's in the minor leagues when Jewels is like in the major league of street smarts."

Johnathan flashed a confused look at Chester.

"Jewels comes across as a shy, quiet, nice girl," continued Chester, returning to his chair, "but you pursued and called my office too many times for me to count. You even called our sweet girl repeatedly, but she cannot return the calls because she is too embarrassed to tell you that she goes to a school for girls who have committed serious crimes! This could be the beginning of a great TV movie! Now, Johnathan decides to take our girl out for an ice cream, which goes well, but now you want to bring her home to meet mama and daddy? Poor Jewels does not have a mama and the only daddy she got is who you are lookin' at."

Johnathan nervously adjusted his posture, sat back on the couch, and remained silent.

"Let me continue. Boy goes to meet her big daddy to ask girl out but big daddy is intimidating and our boy wonders what her big daddy's problem is. It is only a bleeping date! Am I getting warm?"

"Yes . . . sir . . . err . . . something like that."

"Have you talked to your big daddy and big mama yet?" asked Chester. "But your big daddy teaches at a prestigious university. Now, this is where our tragedy gets good. Big daddy has a PhD in English literature; he is white and probably went to Harvard or Stanford. Am I right?"

Johnathan nodded his head and said softly, "Stanford."

"Am I psychic or what . . . but let me continue. They have little Johnathan, the apple of their eye! Johnathan goes to a private school and becomes a scholar and goes to Berkeley, where big daddy teaches. The boy or apple of their eye meets this beautiful child named Jewels, but does he think about her past? Does he hire a private investigator? No, because he's in looooove!"

"It's not like I'm going to marry her," interrupted Johnathan.

"Now that the first intelligent thing I heard from you! So, what do you want?"

"I just thought it would be nice!"

"Nice? You know the old saying 'nice guys finish last'? So why are you trying to finish last in life? Do not waste the poor girl's time! She does not even have a high school diploma! She is trying to pass the GED. She was a major meth user and she paid for her habit by working the streets, and even if she is lucky and she makes it out of this program, where is she going to work? At Macy's? In retail for squat money, and then there is this little thing called color. You are white and she is black and to put it bluntly, do you want little zebras running around your house someday?"

"Come on!" defended Johnathan. "Give me a break. I just want to take her out on a date."

"Okay, how about little raccoons running around? Boy you are heading into some major quagmire and I am trying to help you, cuz I is black and I know what your big daddy would be thinking."

"You are black and your wife is white."

"My wife is educated! My wife is opinionated! My wife is confident and most of all, my wife can take care of herself because her daddy is rich! As for Jewels, she doesn't have a real daddy to take care of her. That was Mr. Pimp's or the drug dealer's game! Again, you are walking into a whole new ball game. Now go home and think about it and talk to your big daddy and good mama and then call me back."

They shook hands and Johnathan walked slowly out of the office.

"Man on the Floor heading for major disaster!" shouted Chester.

Johnathan met Jewels on the porch. She was standing there nervously waiting for the verdict.

"I will call you tonight," said Johnathan. "He didn't say yes or no. I am late for class but I will call you later."

He gave Jewels a hug then walked to the front door, turned around, and waved goodbye.

Jewels followed Johnathan's every movement down the walk to his car. When his car pulled away, her head dropped down and she shook her head and felt the pain of abandonment that was always present in her life.

JEWELS ODOM COMMENTARY #29

You can never tell if Chester is being protective or if he is throwing his weight around just to be the big man on campus thing. You would think that he would jump at the chance to let us girls have a normal life like dating some nice white, black, or brown dude, but no, he has to be this control freak and make it out that the poor guy was going to get raped or something! Maybe he thinks we would do something bad that would make his school or himself look bad? Still, Chester does have a highly protective thing about himself and in many ways, he might be worried that something bad could happen to me around all the white rich folks up in the hills. Whatever his problem, we just keep our mouths shut and hope to hell he isn't going to be some jerk Man on the Floor trying to control our lives and screw up a good thing.

FIFTEEN
More Prunes

Six girls were hanging out on the porch listening to rap music blasting from DJ's ghetto blaster when Mrs. Jackson and her dog Louis exited her house.

"You could set your watch by that old bitch and her damn dog," murmured DJ to herself. "Seven in the morning . . . prunes; lunchtime . . . more prunes; afternoon tea and you guessed it—"

The girls all screamed, "More prunes!"

"You know what I think?" said Kim. "Louis is the one who calls all the shots. That old lady doesn't have a clue. Louis is the one in charge and you can take that to the dog pound, Lassie and whatever!"

"Leave the old lady alone," defended Jewels, repulsed by Kim and DJ's description of Mrs. Jackson. "Remember, she got no one but Louis. We will be there someday."

"For once Jewels is right," intervened Angel. "I would have died if it weren't for my grannie. She raised me when my bitch druggie mother left me." Angel made the sign of the cross and said, "*En el nombre del Padre, el nombre del Hijo, y el nombre del Espíritu Santo. ¡Amén!*"

"And for all you disbelievers, that means 'in the name of the Father, the name of the Son, and the name of the Holy Ghost, Amen!'"

"Let's see if all your Catholic mumbo jumbo stuff works," said DJ, pretending to make the sign of the cross.

DJ left the porch and walked over to Mrs. Jackson and her dog, Louis, who were standing on the sidewalk nearest her house.

"You're a nice dog, yes you are," said DJ. "What's your dog's name? Old Yeller?"

"What did you say?" asked Mrs. Jackson suspiciously. "Sell him? Louis is the best dog you can have. I would never sell him! You be careful girl because Louis doesn't like strangers!"

"Like bite a black girl from juvie?" asked DJ. "Maybe he sees me as a big whopper?"

Louis licked DJ's hand.

"*See*? Louis likes me!" she shouted over to the girls on the porch. "See? He gives me kisses!"

"Come on Louis," said Mr. Jackson angrily. "Let's go for a walk. She wants to sell you! My God, what will be next?"

"Bye Louis, bye Mrs. Jackson." DJ continued in a whisper, "You old bitch. My name is DJ by the way."

Mrs. Jackson turned and gave her a suspicious look and asked angrily, "What did you say?"

Next Anthony appeared on the porch and quickly figured out what was abreast. He asked, "Why do you give that woman a hard time? She represents the past, just like this old mansion. She and the mansion are probably all that's left of the real neighborhood. You should talk with her. She probably has some stories to tell. It's called living history. You know the GED exam does have a history section. It might give you a whole new respect for the past!"

"That lady is so senile that she probably can't remember what she had for breakfast," returned Kim. "Oh yeah, prunes!"

DJ returned and walked slowly up the steps to the school.

Anthony shook his head and was about ready to leave when Louis spotted a cat up the street. Louis, who could barely walk, was rejuvenated by the sight of the cat and pulled away from Mrs. Jackson to run after it.

"Louis you come back here!" she screamed hysterically. "Come back here! Help! Help!"

Louie was about twenty-five yards away when Jewels leaped off the porch and sprinted to get the dog. Louis reached a blind corner and from a distance the loud roar of a garbage truck could be heard approaching.

Jewels went into overdrive, and just as the truck appeared on the corner and was about to hit the old dog, she grabbed the dog's leash and pulled him to safety, out of the reach of the truck. Mrs. Jackson sat down on the curb and buried her face in her hands and cried uncontrollably.

Anthony and a few of the girls went to the woman's side and tried to console her.

"Everything is going to be alright," said Angel in a caring voice. "Are you alright? Can we get you some water?"

Mrs. Jackson stopped crying and shook her head. Soon, Jewels approached with Louis on his leash and passed the leash to Mrs. Jackson, who put her arms around Louis.

"Louis," scolded Mrs. Jackson, "you must never do that again!" Then, she turned to Anthony and explained, "Louie was given to me by my late husband, Thomas, on my birthday. Louis is really all that I have of my late husband and family. My only daughter. . . ." Mrs. Jackson stopped to compose herself and said in a quiet, sad voice, "Amanda was killed last year in a car accident, so Louis is all I have."

The girls remained silent and then turned and walked back to their school. Only Jewels and Anthony remained.

"We are so sorry about your loss," said Anthony seriously. "Are you sure you don't need anything?"

Turning to Jewels, Mrs. Jackson asked, "So, what is your name young lady? You saved Louie's life and mine as well. That was a very brave thing you did!"

"Jewels Odom," she responded.

"Well, Jewels Odom," replied Mrs. Jackson with smile, "someday you must come and visit me and have milk and cookies with me and Louis in my home."

"Okay," replied Jewels, looking over at Anthony. "Yes, I would like that very much."

Anthony helped Mrs. Jackson up, and then Anthony and Jewels walked her and Louis back to her house.

"Girl," said Mrs. Jackson, stopping and turning to Jewels, "when I was your age I was a fast runner too. I used to win all the medals. You ever think of running? You are fast as lightning!"

Jewels only smiled and nodded her head.

Mrs. Jackson departed for her front door, turned, waved, and entered her home.

Anthony remained silent and only nodded his head.

"Shut up!" exclaimed Jewels. "Just shut up . . . and don't get any ideas."

JEWELS ODOM COMMENTARY #30

When I ran from my first foster home I had to survive on the street as a runner delivering pot, working as a look out for drug dealers. I was fast and could outrun the street people who tried to hassle me and get drugs from me. When I became a hooker I could outrun the cops but then I got into speed, crack, etc., and I could barely run a few blocks before I was gasping for air and spitting out blood. After I spent three months in the hall I got my lungs and legs back and now I am pretty much back to about 90 percent. So when old Louis did his thing, my instincts took over, and I was able to save him and do something nice for old lady Jackson. But there was something else that I thought about when I returned the old dog to Mrs. Jackson. It was more about a feeling I had like all the time at this school something was missing. I had moved on from the Man on the Floor BS to something else but I didn't know what was missing, but when I heard Mrs. Jackson speak about her dead daughter and husband, I realized that she was the missing piece that I longed for . . . like what they call old-age wisdom? Here was an educated old black woman who had survived all the death of loved ones and was still doing her thing . . . walking her dog, staying alive. When I looked into her eyes, I saw so much more than what she was saying and I wanted to hear more. I wanted to hear about her long life as a successful, educated black woman. The girls and I don't have anyone like that in our lives, except maybe Angel, who always talked about her 'grannie' . . . something most of us never had and will probably never have. Anyway, Maybe I will take her up her offer on some milk and cookies. You never know!

SIXTEEN

Little Brothers We Wish We Had

The Clark Academy bus pulled to a stop, and one by one, the girls exited the bus in search of the perfect Christmas tree. Anthony followed along, wondering what difficulties he would encounter with the girls choosing *only* one tree. Whenever the girls were given a chance to express their individuality, there was always one major problem: when one said white, the others said black, and when one said hot, the other said cold, and so it went. He assumed the same would take place with the selection of the size and shape of a Christmas tree, and he was right on, particularly with size and shape, because it always turned to penis or willy, although they never actually used the word *penis* in conversation.

Another problem? The girls were dressed in their typical street-walking clothes: high heels, short skirts, teased hair, which of course did not go hand-in-hand with attempting to walk through muddy fields in search of "the perfect tree."

"I warned you about high heels and mud," Anthony said at every turn, "but you had to do it your way."

"Chill," returned Tina. "Chill, man. This is probably the first time I ever had a chance to pick out a real Christmas tree and I needed to dress the part."

The girls were trudging around a muddy field in high heels, looking for the "perfect Christmas tree." When Anthony suggested a medium-sized tree, the girls shook their heads in disgust. When Anthony suggested a very tall tree, the girls all frowned and argued that it wouldn't fit in the study.

"The kind of tree I want has to be sort of short and thin," described DJ, holding her hands close together.

"In your dreams sweetheart," joked Kim. "You know what *Playboy* said about what men like about women. They said our brains. So stop being so physical and use your brain!"

Anthony returned with a saw and the conversation moved back to finding the right tree to fit in their study hall/living room.

Fortunately, two young black kids about eleven or twelve who worked at the tree farm magically appeared and asked if the girls needed any help finding a tree, as well as cutting down the tree. Soon, the two young males fell in line, following the girls around the tree farm like attention-starved puppy dogs.

"We got to get a tree," said DJ, "but that isn't ever goin' happen with this crew."

"Maybe we should just forget the live tree thing and get a fake tree," suggested Tina. "That way everyone will be happy."

They all stopped and stared at Tina. No one said a word until Patricia started singing, "Oh Christmas tree, oh Christmas tree. Tell Tina to go to hell with her artificial tree!"

They finally found the right tree: a large blue spruce that would barely fit into the bus, let alone the school's study hall.

When they were about to vote on the tree, Anthony realized that DJ had disappeared. However, it was not long before he figured out that DJ had gone to the free cider and cookies area.

Soon all the girls moved to the refreshment area and were drinking hot cider when some carolers appeared and the girls joined in singing Christmas carols.

Once the festivities were completed and DJ and the girls had their fill of cider and cookies, the two young male workers loaded the tree into the bus and then asked if the girls wanted them to come to the school to help them unload and decorate the tree.

"Ahhhhhh," commented DJ, "I do not think that would be very cool . . . but if you want to bring presents like a few pizzas, you can come."

"Thanks," said Anthony to the young males, "but we can handle it."

"Come on," lectured Jewels. "These young, strong boys helped us find the tree and they want to help bring the tree home. Come on, let's vote on it. How many think Joey and Frankie, our two strong, handsome boys, should come back to school with us and help us decorate the tree and sing carols?"

The girls unanimously all agreed to have the two boys come back to the school with them.

"Okay," said Anthony. "I'm sure Chester won't mind."

The two boys, who by now had developed serious crushes on some of the girls, squeezed between DJ on one side and Kim and Patricia on the other side as they rode the bus to school with the girls.

On the way home, they all sang carols.

Patricia commented, "This is like having a real family with a bunch of sisters, and let's not forget our little brothers."

The boys only blushed at all the attention they were receiving from their new, young black sisters.

A sense of stillness came over the bus and for the thirty-minute drive back to the school, few words were expressed. It was as if they had processed what Jewels had said about family and it was being fully appreciated.

When they all returned to the school, they spent the remainder of the night decorating the house and tree. After they finished decorating, they drank apple cider, ate cookies, and then sang more carols.

On the drive back to their homes, Frankie commented to Anthony that the school and girls were pretty cool. "Only I think I saw a few of them on San Pablo Avenue once when I got out late from a movie. I mean they dressed like they were movie stars! Is this a school for girls who want to be in the movies?" he asked seriously.

"Well," said Anthony with a smile, "you never know."

JEWELS ODOM COMMENTARY #31

It is sad to see the girls look at every outing as a chance to show their wares. They know no other way, but I think Anthony hopes that within these girls' heads a positive person will appear from their troubled past lives. He can always demand a strict dress code, but that will only make us hate the Man on the Floor even more. He has to accept us girls for who we are. I think Chester knows this, which is why Chester doesn't make the dress code a big deal. For Anthony, either he's too chicken or maybe smart enough not to push it. If these girls feel the need to dress up when they leave the school grounds, then they should go for it.

SEVENTEEN

When You Don't Have a Future?

"Again, I want to thank you for saving Louis from that garbage truck that always speeds around our street corner," said Mrs. Jackson, speaking to Jewels over a cup of hot chocolate and cookies. Jewels had periodically stopped by to check up on how she was doing since her rescue of Louis. They had formed a symbolic grandmother–granddaughter relationship, something Jewels had never experienced, and it provided a closeness that Mrs. Jackson seriously missed since she had lost her daughter in a car crash a year ago.

"All I have are a bunch of memories and, of course, dear Louis and my house. You know they have been trying to get me to sell, offering me ungodly sums of money . . . those damn realtors! They want me to sell so they can tear this house down and build one of those big ones down the street. Sad, but all that is left of the real neighborhood is your school and my house. You girls were lucky to get the old mansion. As much as I was afraid when you girls moved in because of gangs and drugs, I am so happy the realtors did not get hold of it."

Jewels nodded her head and focused on Mrs. Jackson's every word. When Mrs. Jackson spoke, her hands would twitch until she would clasp them together to stop the twitching. Jewels avoided focusing on her hands, always looking directly at her expressive face for fear of making her self-conscious. Still, because she was in her seventies, Jewels worried about the twitch and would ask about her health and whether she had regular health checkups.

Mrs. Jackson ignored Jewels's questions about her health, always redirecting the conversation to food or to her late husband or daughter.

"Would you like another cookie?" she asked. "My husband, Thomas, loved my cookies! It has been so long since I have been around someone your age. When I lost my dear Amanda, I did not want to talk to anyone, especially teenagers. It was just too painful."

"Sure, another cookie and some milk would be great," replied Jewels.

Mrs. Jackson left the room and soon returned with a plate of cookies. Then she walked to the living room, picked up a box, and returned to the table.

"Remember, I told you that I used to be a runner," she said proudly and then pulled out some old bronze track medals that were in a box on the table.

"I got this in high school," she explained, passing a medal to Jewels. "First place . . . the 100-yard dash . . . two years in a row!"

Mrs. Jackson took out another trophy from a box.

"Here's my favorite trophy," she said with obvious pride. "I got a first place in the 440-county high school track meet. I saw you run the other day and girl you got it all. You need to run in meets! Really!"

"Well, maybe someday, I mean, if I can go to college." Then Jewels laughed sarcastically and said, "Imagine me in college! That would be a joke."

"Can I tell you something personal?" asked Mrs. Jackson, looking intensely at Jewels. "I do not mean any disrespect, but I noticed it right away when I saw you girls on the first day when you all got off your old bus. You did not run like some wild animal like the rest of them, but you stopped and looked at the old mansion, almost giving respect it. I felt there was something different about you from the rest, and then you saved Louis from getting run over by that garbage truck. No, I know people, and you remind me a lot of my daughter, God rest her soul."

"Thank you," said Jewels, embarrassed. Jewels stopped for a moment, took a deep breath, and then took a dress from a bag she was holding. "I need a favor from you."

"Yes?"

"Well, one of our girls got asked to go to a dinner party at this boy's home. It will be a fancy dinner and she must wear this dress, but it needs some work. There's a rumor that you are good with a needle and thread?"

"I am not sure where that rumor started, but I am not bad. Sure, I can help. But . . . would that girl happen to be you?"

"Well . . . errr yes," replied Jewels "Maybe I should have been honest, but I was embarrassed or something like that. This dress is too long. My social worker gave it me."

"Okay," said Mrs. Jackson, getting a measuring tape from a nearby drawer. "We need to measure the hem, so you will need to stand on a chair."

Jewel climbed up on the chair while Mrs. Jackson went about addressing the hem line to fit Jewels's long, shapely legs.

"Yep, you got a runner's legs. You really need to think about competing."

"Thank you," said Jewels. "Yes, I will think about it."

"Just because I agreed to help you does not mean I like all of you girls. That loud, filthy music they play and smoking! I am doing this because I owe you a favor for saving my dog—that's all."

Mrs. Jackson continued with her measuring, but every so often she would stop and turn away before composing herself again.

"I'm really sorry," she said, "but I get very emotional because I did this once for my daughter, Amanda, when she went to her high school prom."

Mrs. Jackson wiped a tear off her cheek and continued measuring the hem line.

Jewels climbed off the chair and was about to hug her, but stepped back, afraid she would be rejected.

"Now girl, be very careful because you will tear the stitching."

Mrs. Jackson walked over to a nearby desk drawer and took out a small box.

"Here is a little something you can wear," she whispered holding two golden earrings in her hands. "They're my special earrings and necklace that my dear husband, Thomas, gave me. God bless his soul. He gave them to me on our fiftieth wedding anniversary. These jewels would have been for dear Amanda."

Jewels moved closer to Mrs. Jackson, paused for a moment, and quickly gave her a big hug and a kiss on the cheek.

Mrs. Jackson became visibly uncomfortable, but quickly composed herself and said sternly, "Try to get home at a reasonable hour so you do not wake Louis and me and be careful with the stitching."

JEWELS ODOM COMMENTARY #32

Toni has always said to us, "It's hard to have a present if you don't have a past," and I always say, "If you don't have a present or a past, you don't have a future!" Mrs. Jackson represents a past and a present to me and in many ways she gives me the confidence that I could have a future as well.

EIGHTEEN
Never a Time for Coke!

"Glad to see that you're reading *People* magazine," said Ms. Sawyer, the county parole officer for the Clark Academy. "How about something a bit more challenging or more academic like the classics?"

DJ jumped up from her bed and shouted angrily, "See, you don't even know what you're talkin' about! The GED takes questions from these magazines. So, misssssss smarty pants, if you don't believe me, then talk to our teacher!"

"Well," said Ms. Sawyer, "I learn something every day, but miss smarty pants, when you read the classics, the vocabulary is not on the level of a third grader."

Sawyer turned to Sonya, who was lying in her bed, ignoring the conversation between Sawyer and DJ.

"Don't say hello, Sonya," said Sawyer, feeling the tenseness in the room.

Sonya, an eighteen-year-old black girl with long, yellow-streaked black hair, shared the room with DJ.

Toni stood in the doorway like a security guard, while Sawyer walked suspiciously around the room as if she were investigating a crime. She walked over to the dresser and picked up a brush and comb and placed them down.

"Growing your hair out, I see?" asked Sawyer with a discerning smile.

"If you say so," said Sonya, not looking up from her magazine.

Sawyer moved to the closet.

"The last program you were in, I believe you bombed out of it?" questioned Sawyer. "I hope you're not thinking of running or doing something stupid. You don't have any more chances. Do you mind if I see your wardrobe?"

"Suit yourself," said Sawyer. "No pun intended."

Sawyer opened the door and looked in and touched a wool sweater.

"Nice . . . a gift?" she questioned.

"No," returned Sonya. "Goodwill."

"Touché," Sawyer replied smugly.

Sawyer bent down and picked up some shoes, shook them, and out fell a folded piece of paper. She opened the paper, smelled it, and then tasted it.

"Goddamn it, Sonya," yelled Toni. "Not coke!"

"I've never seen that before," defended Sonya. "It's a set up! It is not mine!"

Sawyer turned to Toni. "Now, where did I hear that before? Like I said, I'm just doing my job."

Thirty minutes later, a tearful Sonya was taken out of the Clark Academy in handcuffs by two police officers. The girls stood on the porch watching silently as Sonya was led to a police car. The girls watched with sober expressions as the police car slowly pulled away.

Chester walked out to the porch and exclaimed sarcastically, "Once a cokie, always a cokie."

He shook his head and walked back into the mansion. When he passed Toni, he responded coldly, "Well that opens a space for the girl from Pittsburgh who is on the waiting list. You need to call her social worker. Oh well," he repeated, "once a cokie, always a cokie!"

JEWELS ODOM COMMENTARY #33

Everyone knew that Sonya was usin', but no one wanted to be a snitch. When anyone confronted Sonja, she would only say, "Shut the fuck up. I never had a mother and I sure as hell don't need one now!"

The only drug that is going down with the girls is pot. I stay away from hard drugs but some of the girls hope the staff will get loose and they could maybe go out and get some hard stuff. Their homeboys always find a way, like hiding it in the neighborhood. They come around late at night so no one sees them and then leave the stuff at a special spot on the street. I mean you can always sneak out on

Mary, our 11 p.m. to 7 a.m. night shift staff, because if she catches us, we pretend we are going out to the front porch for a smoke. Still, getting drugs is a piece of cake, or as Chester always says, "Once a cokie, always a cokie!"

NINETEEN

Colonel Sanders and Road Warrior!

A black official military car pulled up in front of the Clark Academy. An older man in his early thirties dressed in military garb was driving the car. He got out and opened the back door as another serious-looking military man in his late forties climbed out. The driver moved to the other side of the car and opened the rear door. A tall, white girl, about seventeen years old, dressed in tawdry-looking clothes appeared. She wore torn Levi pants and a black hoodie. Dark eye shadow surrounded her eyes, which almost made her look like a raccoon. She had earrings in her nose and ears while a black dotted tattoo ran up and down her hands. She wore an angry expression on her face that said, *Fuck your world!*

"Please wait for us," ordered the officer to the driver. "I am not sure how long this will take."

"Andrea," the officer said curtly, "our appointment with Dr. Barkley is for 3:00 p.m. I only have thirty minutes and then I need to return to base."

Andrea made no response. She looked down at the pavement while the officer began to walk up the driveway.

"I said we only have thirty minutes. I am not going to play games with you. Now let's go!"

Finally, Andrea began to move slowly toward the porch.

Patricia, who was hanging out on the porch, ignored the two visitors and yelled to herself, "I hate these bullshit rules. Why am I being down-graded? I didn't do nothin'!"

When Patricia spied Andrea with her tattoos and her father in military garb, she shook her head in disgust at the sight of the two and walked to the other end of the porch to have a smoke while casting a cold stare at Andrea and her father.

The officer and his daughter walked into the school and met DJ bombing down the stairs.

"Whoaaaa mama!" yelled a shocked DJ. "Trick or treat, smell my feet. Give me something good to eat. If you don't, I will pull down your underwear!"

"Please tell Dr. Barkley that Colonel Parker and his daughter, Andrea, are here," commanded the colonel.

"Yo Chester! Check this out!" roared DJ to the upstairs hallway. "You got some interesting visitors and it ain't even Halloween!"

Moments later Chester appeared at the top of the stairway.

"I mean," continued DJ, "you got Colonel Sanders and his daughter road warrior here to see you!"

"Girl!" shouted Chester. "I told you what would happen if you kept eating all that Kentucky fried grease! Now, why are you screamin' like some banshee? If you want them to take you away, I can arrange that. Now what is all this psych unit yelling for?"

Chester walked to the top of the stairway and saw the colonel and his daughter.

"Oh, yes," said Chester, embarrassed. "Colonel, please excuse DJ. She's not used to visitors. Are you, DJ? Please come on up. DJ is just having one of her daily 'I need attention' attacks!"

The colonel and his daughter climbed the stairs and the three disappeared into Chester's office. Thirty minutes later, Chester, Colonel Parker, and Andrea appeared downstairs. Chester shook Colonel Parker's hand.

"Andrea will be in good hands, Colonel," encouraged Chester, looking pointedly at Andrea, who only stared at the floor. Colonel Parker shook Chester's hand and then looked sternly at Andrea.

"I expect you to behave," he said sternly. "You don't have any more chances left. I cannot send you to any more military schools. This is the end of the road, missy."

The colonel departed as Toni appeared from the kitchen.

"This must be Andrea. I am Toni, Chester's lovely wife and counseling director. Are you hungry, dear? The poor girl is all skin and bones."

"She looks well fed to me," quipped Chester, evaluating Andrea. "Now don't start babying the child!"

Andrea shook her head.

"See? She's not hungry," said Chester. "Isn't that right, Andrea?"

JEWELS ODOM COMMENTARY #34

I have seen girls like Andrea at the hall, mostly for using drugs or simply as runaways. They often come from homes that are unlike most of ours, like the projects, which were dominated by poor black people or drug-addicted black folks. When I talk to some of these military kids, most say that they got tired of always moving around and never staying in one place . . . different schools . . . couldn't make friends, and worse, their fathers treat them like they are in the military. They say they have so many rules that they never know which way to turn. When they come into the hall, they have the black tats and the dress is mostly gothic. They never look you straight in the eye and their hair always covers up their faces. Andrea is no different. Bottom line, for all of us—it comes d own to trust or lack thereof.

TWENTY

It Never Leaves You!

Jewels was having the same frightening dream that she had had so many times before. She was twelve years old, living in a foster home. One older boy was holding her down while another was trying to tear off her clothes. She struggled and screamed, but no one came to her rescue. However, she always woke up before her clothes were torn off.

This night Jewels found herself in a corner of her bedroom, crying and shivering uncontrollably.

"Are you all right, Jewels?" asked Angel, touching her gently. "It's me, Angel. Are you okay?"

"Yeah," said Jewels in a dazed and incoherent voice. "I should not have had that cake before I went to bed. Next time I'll give it to DJ."

Bonita walked into the room.

"What the hell is goin' on?" asked Bonita, concerned. "You nearly scared the living shit out of me!"

"Come on, baby," comforted Angel. "You were only having a bad dream."

"I said I'm all right!" cried Jewels, pulling away.

Angel pulled back, crooning in Spanish, "You can't keep everything in. Let it out."

Jewels climbed back into her bed and crawled under the covers, trying to hide until everyone left; then she stuck her head out again.

"What the hell?" muttered Angel. "I was just trying to help!"

"Shit," said Bonita. "Now, I'm awake and I can't get to sleep without taking my meds!"

DJ walked in and asked, "What's all the commotion? By the way, did you guys finish off the cake that was left over from dinner? It's my medication and its helps me sleep."

The girls ignored DJ and returned to Jewels.

Jewels turned her back on Angel, saying quietly and in a sincere voice, "I know. I know. It's just I have always had to do it on my own. There was never anyone around when I had those dreams in the past."

Jewels pulled the covers over her head and remained quiet.

JEWELS ODOM COMMENTARY #35

I don't care how much therapy you get. The memory of rape never leaves you because you were helpless. You were alone and there was no one there to help you. It goes back to when I was a baby and my mother was always zonked out on drugs. I would lie in that crib for hours with a wet diaper or poop and there was no one there to change me. I would cry and cry, but no one ever came. The same thing happened with rape. I yelled for help and no one ever came.

TWENTY-ONE

Sister of the Streets!

The large, stately mansion was filled with East Bay's dignitaries and a few donors to support a camp scholarship program for troubled children. At the dining table sat Johnathan Simon, talking to a guest, while a very nervous Jewels studied the silverware, going over in her mind which silverware to use first. Johnathan sat next to her and tried to start up a conversation, but Jewels remained quiet with a demeanor that stated, *What the hell am I doing here?*

A middle-aged white attorney named Cole Davis sat across the table from Jewels and stared intensely at her. Jewels shyly returned his look until they both realized where they had seen each other before. When he took a piece of shrimp, seductively sucking on it, Jewels turned abruptly from him, stood up, not escaping from the man's stares until Johnathan stood up from the table and suggested to Jewels, "If you need to use the bathroom, it is just down the hall."

Jewels offered a nervous "thank you" and moved quickly toward the bathroom.

Minutes later, Cole Davis got up from the table and moved to the women's bathroom and waited for Jewels to reappear from the bathroom.

A few minutes later, Jewels appeared and Cole Davis quickly confronted her. "I'm not going to make a scene, honey, but I really need to talk to you."

Jewels tried to ignore him but he persisted and was about to grab her arm when Jewels said, "Okay, but only a minute."

"Follow me," ordered Cole Davis.

He led Jewels into a secluded pantry off the kitchen and took out his wallet, flashing a hundred-dollar bill.

"Sweetheart," he said moving closer to Jewels. "I missed you on the streets. Look, nobody will ever know. How about a little quickie and we both win?"

"You fucking asshole!" yelled Jewels, pushing him away. "I'm a student now getting my high school diploma and I will never have to be a hoe again."

"Don't get uppity with me, you little whore," he said, moving closer to her. "I knew you before little Johnathan started dicking you. The only graduation you'll ever see is my dick in your mouth."

He lunged at her, but she pushed him away. He returned and grabbed her, trying to kiss her.

"Leave me alone, asshole!" she screamed, trying to fight him off. When he slipped and fell to the floor, Jewels ran out of the pantry and raced to the front door and out of the house.

Johnathan continued to sit at the table with a concerned look. Finally, he got up and began searching for Jewels. In his search, he found Cole Davis still in the pantry.

"You looking for your bitch?" he asked, adjusting his sport coast. "She went out the front door. My money is no longer good enough for that bitch. Remember, when you kiss her, you kiss every dick in town."

Johnathan grabbed Cole Davis by his coat and pushed him against a side wall.

"If you have hurt her in any way," Johnathan threatened, "I'll deal with you later!"

Johnathan headed for the front entrance but ran into a friend of his father who tried to start up a conversation with him.

Jewels was still outside on the front lawn looking disoriented and not knowing which direction to run. Johnathan finally broke away from the dinner guest.

"I'm sorry sir," he said to the guest, "but I have to check on someone."

"Youth . . . always in a rush," responded the guest. "But if you are looking for that beautiful young lady, she's headed out to the front lawn or driveway."

Johnathan ran to the driveway and confronted a parking attendant.

"Did a black-haired girl in a white dress go this way?"

"Yes sir, only a few minutes ago. She went in that direction," stated the attendant, pointing toward the long, winding driveway.

Jewels took off her high-heeled shoes and ran past a row of luxurious cars and then through a neighborhood of expensive homes. She continued down through another neighborhood, and finally after about a mile, she was back down in the crime-ridden world of the flatlands and downtown Oakland where druggies came out of the darkness and tried to pull at her for money. A group of street hookers standing on the corner began to laugh at her in her torn dress and no shoes.

"Hey, Cinderella!" yelled one hooker, "you better clean up your act if you're lookin' for prince charming, cuz it ain't goin' to happen here!"

She passed a man who was dry humping a woman against a car while another group of street people passed around a joint.

Jewels, tired and tearful, tried to escape the Oakland streets. Hooker Wanda finally spied Jewels walking aimlessly through the rain and cold.

"Girl," scolded Wanda, "you look like hell! Are you in trouble?"

Jewels pulled away and continued to walk swiftly down Oakland's San Pablo Avenue, a haven for street walkers and druggies.

"Don't be stupid, girl" yelled Wanda. "I have a borrowed car. It's over there. I will drive you home, honey."

Wanda quickly led Jewels away to a beat-up old Chevy.

"Quick," ordered Wanda, "get in before my asshole pimp comes!"

Wanda opened the passenger door and helped Jewels in the car. Then she walked around to the other side and quickly got in just before a drunk appeared from the darkness and tried to open the car door, but Wanda quickly locked the door before he could get in.

The drunk reached down for a brick to break the window as Wanda stepped on the accelerator and peeled off.

"These fuckin' johns are not worth the air they breathe," she said angrily. She rubbed Jewels's back, who was curled up like a fetus on the front seat. "Now you just tell me where you live honey and I'll drive you there."

"2093 . . . Clark Street," stuttered Jewels, "up in the hills."

"High rollers up in that area," exclaimed Wanda, her eyes studying the road. "I have been here, done this hood before. Well," she continued, "you lucked out tonight with old Wanda. Another night you could have been hurt, maybe worse."

Jewels nodded her head and then blew on her hands and tried to stay warm.

At school, Toni, Chester, DJ, and the rest of the girls were sitting around a table drinking milk, eating cookies, and reading magazines when Johnathan bolted into the study/living room looking stressed out. His black tie dangled from his shirt collar and his face was flushed.

"Did Jewels come home?" he asked emotionally. "She left the party alone! She was upset! I think some guest set her off and said something insulting to her. I drove my car all over Oakland looking for her, but she disappeared. I'm really worried she's in trouble!"

"It will not be the first time and it will not be the last," said Chester. "I believe I did warn you."

Minutes later, the front door opened and Jewels and Wanda entered the living room. Jewels's beautiful dress was torn and covered with mud. Her hair was tangled and her mascara was smeared across her face. She spotted Johnathan, saying apologetically, "I am so sorry," and ran upstairs to her bedroom, crying.

Johnathan ran to the bottom of the stairs and yelled, "I am so sorry, Jewels! It was all my fault!"

Angel left and ran upstairs to console Jewels.

Toni put her arm around Johnathan and explained, "It is not your fault. It's hard to lose your past when you are trying to be in the present."

Wanda was standing in the corner alone until Chester walked up to her.

"Don't be shy," said Chester, "I am Dr. Barkley and welcome to the Clark Academy. On behalf of all our students, we want to thank you for helping Jewels."

"I have been in Jewels's shoes before," explained Wanda. "My name is Wanda Jacobs."

"Would you like some coffee?" Toni asked. "How about some cookies?"

"No thank you," Wanda returned. "I think I better be going. Just tell Jewels to stay the course."

The girls all watched as Wanda moved to the front door and left.

"Well," Toni said, "always remember: you can't judge a book by its cover."

Ten minutes later, Jewels appeared in the study/living room in a bathrobe. Her face was cleaned and her hair was neatly combed.

"Well," said Jewels to Johnathan, "we will have to give it a try another time."

Jewels and Johnathan both looked over at Chester, who nodded his head, "I will let my lovely wife decide."

"When the going gets tough, the tough get going," Toni said with a smile.

JEWELS ODOM COMMENTARY #36

Our pasts are like a rerun movie that appears when we least expect it.

When my rerun movie appeared at the dinner party, it was amazing how quickly I returned to my old survival ways. In this case there was the "john" and the very wealthy and educated people who said, "You don't belong. You are not one of us." And my escape was to run like I was running from the cops on the Oakland streets, and where did I end up but back on the streets, and look who I was escaping from now: the pimps, the johns, the hoes, the drug addicts, and look who saved me: Wanda, who was a sister of the streets. Yet this time, I had a place to go to and that was with my sisters at the Clark Academy, something I never had before.

TWENTY-TWO
His Sacred Cow

Jewels left her bedroom wearing a long bathrobe and encountered Angel, Patricia, and Kim, who were only wearing bras and panties. They were in the upstairs bathroom dancing to music from a ghetto blaster and the girls pretended to be strippers, demonstrating a variety of provocative moves.

"Come on, Jewels," prodded Kim, gyrating to the music. "You just might get a job someday as a stripper, but only if you get more on top!" Kim pushed up her boobs and continued gyrating. "You need to exercise your booty," she said playfully. "If you snooze, you lose what used to be good!" She shook her behind and started singing, "Take it off baby. Take it all off!"

"I would like to take a shower and take a dump," Jewels answered, frustrated. "I haven't showered in days!"

"Gee, thanks, Jewels, for the play by play," responded Kim, not missing a beat in her gyrations.

The girls ignored Jewels and continued their provocative dancing. Jewels looked at the tattoo on Angel's neck and then shook her head in disgust. Angel responded to Jewels's facial expression, "Bitch, you got a problem with my tats?" Then she continued in Spanish, "*Entiendes* means 'do you fuckin' understand?'"

"And Manuel?" asked Jewels, not intimidated by Angel's outburst. "Who the fuck is Manuel? Some loser? And why does Mr. Manuel macho man need to brand his sacred cow with his name?"

"Since when did you come into my fuckin' life?" she yelled in Jewels's face.

"You and I are human beings," returned Jewels, not backing down. "You and I share a room. You and I need to talk. You and I are trying to survive. *Entiendes?* See? I speak Spanish too."

"Okay," said Angel, staring intensely at Jewels. "I can play the 'you and I' ghetto game too."

"And so how do you want to begin?" asked Jewels.

"This is how I want to begin. He's dead and I'm alive, but all I have of him is this bullet hole in my body." Angel pulled up her shirt to show a two-inch scar on the side of her abdomen. "I'm tryin' to get on with my life, but people like you keep reminding me the game is like the past . . . like he's dead. End of the 'you and me' ghetto game. So my tat helps me remember him. Case closed. Now leave me the fuck alone!"

"I'm really sorry," said Jewels in a sincere voice. "I didn't know. You and me share a room. I already explained to you that this is not ghetto time to me."

"Okay, one time only," said Angel, frustrated. "One time only. I stabbed a girl in a fight and now I got a restitution charge that I will never be able to pay off. I must pay her medical bills. Any more stupid questions? Or maybe you want to donate to the Angel payback fund!"

Jewels stepped back and said sincerely, "I'm sorry . . . really sorry to hear that. Well, get out and open up your dream beauty salon and pay it back."

Jewels held out her hand to make peace. Angel looked at Jewels suspiciously and then reached out and shook her hand.

Jewels turned to a mirror and began combing her hair. "Maybe you can cut this back a little?" she asked with a smile.

"Yeah, but for a price!" said Angel. "Like I said, I got this restitution charge, but since we are roomies, it will be a freebie. See me tomorrow after school."

JEWELS ODOM COMMENTARY #37

We all have a history of junk stuck inside our brains that wants to come out, but we are too afraid to deal with it. Our lives are like a muddy slope that you have to climb up each day, one step at a time, always afraid that you will fall and slide back down, never knowing that you can get back up and try again!

TWENTY-THREE

No Pussy Votes!

The girls were all crammed into Bonita and Patricia's bedroom. A candle sat alone in the center of the room, giving off faint light that reflected off of the girls' faces, accentuating the seriousness of the situation.

"The meeting will now begin," announced Tina, holding a flashlight. "Remember the rules: Nobody talks, unless they have the flashlight, and there can be no wolfing and remember to keep your voices down. Pimply faced Mary will be doing night rounds in forty-five minutes. We do not want her old pimply face up here. Okay? Now Bonita, tell us your problem. Remember we are not here to judge. We are only her to listen and support your decision."

"My asshole social worker visited me the other day and told me I needed to give up custody of my three kids," said Bonita tearfully. "There's this rich black doctor and his white wife who want to adopt all my babies or none at all. They have this big house in Piedmont. You know, great backyard, great schools, not the fucked-up life I would give to them."

Kim mimicked Bonita and said, "Yeah, great life . . . definitely a couple of Oreos. Either he doesn't have the sperm or she don't like the screamin! This is bullshit. I say fuck them. All these Oreos are stealing our babies. I say fuck 'em!"

"Goddamn it," whispered Tina. "Lower your fuckin' voice."

"They've have had them now for six months," continued Bonita. "It's a foster adopt program."

When Bonita began to cry uncontrollably, Jasmine put her arms around Bonita. "Bonita, you got to do what's best for your kids," explained Tina. "But it's your call and ain't nobody else's."

"Ssshhhhh," interrupted Patricia. "Bonita, you got to be quiet or that bitch Mary will be up here. So, what the hell should she do? Again, you said you would agree on what we come up with," said Patricia, who then looked around at all the girls, "Like it's time. We need to vote on what she should do."

"Okay," explained Tina. "Let's vote on these slips of paper. This gives us the chance to vote the way we feel and not what others tell you to do. 'Yes' if she should give them up or 'no' if she should keep them and you can't be a pussy's and not want to vote."

"Abstain," interrupted Kim. "It means to not vote."

"Fuck you with your big words," returned Patricia. "They all mean the same. Pussy vote is a pussy vote."

Tina passed out slips of paper and pencils and after about five minutes of serious contemplation, the girls voted and returned the slips to Tina, who began to count the votes slowly.

"The verdict is almost unanimous," said Patricia. "All voted that she should keep her kids, except one pussy voted that she should give them up."

All the girls looked over at Jewels, who was looking dead serious.

Bonita got up slowly and walked out of the room, dejected and confused.

Patricia looked at Jewels and said, "Asshole. It should have been all of us. You needed to show her that we *all* back her."

"She lost those kids the minute she started using," replied Jewels angrily. "Give me a fucking break. She would have lost them anyway through neglect or whatever our so-called mothers or fathers couldn't give us. At least they got a chance now. Look at us! We needed adoption. I would never have gone to the streets if I had had a home. Wake up! She has got to save her kids. Give them a chance in life."

Jewels got up angrily and threw a pencil against the bedroom wall and left the group.

"I hear noise up there," yelled Mary from the bottom of the stairs, "and it better be the mice and not you girls. Now get to bed or I will pull all of you up!"

JEWELS ODOM COMMENTARY #38

These girls are still stuck in their pasts that led them to the streets to survive. Maybe if we had been adopted into a real family and not placed in foster care or residential treatment, we would never have run to the streets and could have avoided rape and even being molested. Bonita understands what is at stake and I believe she chose the right path instead of a future path to the streets.

A week later, Bonita was hiding behind a large maple tree watching a white mother and black father playing with three young black children in a large, grassy backyard with elaborate playground equipment. The father pushed one girl, about five years old, on a swing, and the mother played with the two younger children on a slide. The children's laughter and screams could be heard throughout the neighborhood. Bonita continued to stand behind a tree watching intensely from a distance.

She dropped down to her knees and began to cry uncontrollably. She tried to control her deep, loud sobs, which echoed from behind the tree. She stayed on her knees, holding onto the tree as if she were holding one of her children, and remained rooted in that position for a few more minutes until the parents took the three children into the house.

Two hours later, Bonita was in a dilapidated old house shooting up heroin. A black male was sitting on the floor in a corner drugged out of his mind.

In another area of Oakland, Mrs. Jackson sat in the driver's seat of a late-model car, barely able to see over the steering wheel as she cautiously guided the car through the back streets of Oakland. Her dog Louis was sitting on the front seat next to DJ. Jewels and Angel sat in the back seat slowly giving directions to Mrs. Jackson.

"When was the last time Louis had a bath?" asked DJ holding his nose. "Man, Louis, you will never get a woman with a smell like that!"

Mrs. Jackson intervened angrily: "Leave Louis alone! It is not his fault. He's just got bad teeth, something you youngins' don't know anything about yet."

Angel asked, "Is this as fast as this jalopy goes?"

"Daisy is goin' as fast as she can go," defended Mrs. Jackson. "She's old, but she's been a good friend to me, just like Louis. I just do not know what I would do without them both. You children don't know how hard it is for a person my age to lose family and friends. Do you know how many close friends I have lost just in the past year? Well, too many to talk about. Oh, the pain! Thank God for Louis! He is all I got! And Daisy well—"

Jewels interrupted and said, "Excuse me, but you need to take a left here. No! Not right! Left! That is right! I mean good."

Mrs. Jackson nearly hit a parked car, yet she still seemed relaxed and focused.

"I think maybe we should call the police," she said driving carefully. "That's why I pay all those taxes! Do you want to know how much I used to pay in taxes when Thomas was alive? God rest his soul."

"No . . . please," returned Jewels seriously, "we cannot call the police because they will take Bonita back to the hall." Jewels continued surveying the street. "That's the place, over there! I would know that hole anywhere. Please pull over there."

Mrs. Jackson cautiously pulled in front of a dilapidated abandoned house. The windows were boarded up and an abandoned car sat in the front yard.

"I cannot imagine any human being living in a place like that!" exclaimed Mrs. Jackson.

"Angel, you stay with Mrs. Jackson, and DJ, you come with me," ordered Jewels. "We don't know who is in the house and how they could react to us."

"I think there might be rats and stuff in the place," warned DJ. "Maybe I should stay and protect Angel, who is protecting Mrs. Jackson and Louis."

"Stop fooling around," whispered Jewels, getting out of the car. "We don't have any time if she is using."

Jewels and DJ moved to the house and tried to push the front door open, but it was locked, so they went around to the side of the house. A tied-up pit bull began to bark viciously at the two girls. They found a door slightly ajar and followed a dim light to where they found a black man about thirty-five years old lying unconscious on a mattress. His eyes were rolled back and he had drool dripping from his mouth.

Jewels grabbed the man by his shirt and pulled him up.

"Where's Bonita?" she screamed. "Where the fuck is Bonita, you low-life?"

"Baby . . . baby," repeated the semi-conscious man.

Jewels let go of the man and ran to a back room and found Bonita semi-conscious on a mattress. A needle was on the floor nearby. Jewels felt for Bonita's pulse but quickly realized she had no pulse and frantically banged on her chest. When Bonita showed no response, she applied mouth-to-mouth resuscitation.

"Wake up, Bonita! Bonita, wake up!" she yelled, banging on her chest. "I hate you! Wake up! Do not leave your kids! They still need you! Please Bonita, wake up. Your kids need you! Wake up!"

DJ walked over to Jewels and tried to pull her away, but Jewels only pushed DJ away and continued to bang on Bonita's chest.

"It's fucking over!" yelled DJ. "Give it up! You can't save her!"

"No! No!" screamed Jewels. "Leave me alone!"

Jewels placed her head on Bonita's chest and cried uncontrollably.

"We need to call 911," DJ said, calmly looking around for a phone. She moved to another room and found a phone that surprisingly worked.

"A girl has OD'd on heroin!" she shouted to the operator. "We need help. We are at 234 East 67th St. Please hurry!"

JEWELS ODOM COMMENTARY #39

The shadow of death is always very close to all of us: a gang shooting, OD on drugs, a pimp's beating. So how do you explain Bonita's pain and her response to losing her three kids? How do you choose between a life with your kids and poverty or a life for your kids with a future? We all came to such crossroads in our lives as Bonita had to face. I know I voted for her kids' future; still, if they were my kids, I might have chosen a different path.

Bonita's corpse lay in an open, plain coffin. The faces of Bonita's three children, the foster-adoptive parents, and the mostly black congregation reflected the gravity of the situation.

Sitting behind the family was the Clark Academy contingency, who were all dressed in black: Toni, Anthony, Jewels, DJ, Jamie, and Mrs. T. The rest of the guests included social workers, school psychologists, and Clark Academy staff, who sat in an adjacent pew.

Bonita's three children and their foster parents walked to the coffin. The children followed the directions of their foster parents and knelt next to the coffin and prayed silently.

One by one, the mother picked up each child and helped them place a white rose on Bonita's chest. Next, the Clark Academy girls filed past the casket, placing more roses on Bonita's chest. Finally, Angel placed a photo of Bonita's children into the casket.

Jewels was the last to go to the casket. Her loud cries echoed throughout church. When she knelt down, her head dropped down and rested against the casket, and she remained in this position for a long time. Finally, Toni and DJ went to Jewels and slowly walked her away from the casket and back to the pew. Jewels sat for a few minutes and finally, with the help of Toni, exited the chapel with all the Clark Academy students.

As the Clark Academy bus pulled away, Jewels continued to stare at the church until tears began to run down her cheeks. She had a flashback of a funeral she had attended for a girlfriend who had been killed in a gang shooting when she was fourteen years old. Jewels's body quivered as if she were trying to escape the memory of her friend's body lying in the casket, but when she came to her senses again, she could only see Bonita lying in her casket.

"Hey Jewels," asked DJ, "you okay?"

At first Jewels didn't respond, but then slowly, nodded her head.

The girls returned to school and placed a vase of flowers on Bonita's desk.

Later in the day Anthony read a poem to the girls called "No Man Is an Island," by John Donne. The poem hit home, particularly with Jewels, who thanked Anthony for reading the poem to the girls.

"I reread the poem a number of times to myself," she explained to Anthony. "What I came away with was the last line: 'And therefore, never send to know for whom the bell tolls; it tolls for thee.' I would say the poem expressed what we all felt with Bonita's death except instead of the title 'No Man Is an Island,' I would change it to 'No Woman Is an Island' but that might be too weird."

JEWELS ODOM COMMENTARY #40

Most of us have never read much stuff in our life. Again, only those stupid magazines about celebs and so forth. But the more Anthony exposed us to literature like the poem "No Man is an Island" it not only made us think but it went to our hearts. After he read the poem, some of us cried a little. I think us girls realize that reading this stuff was healing which is why I think everyone stayed pretty much to themselves the rest of the day. There were no fights or wolfing matches. Thank you Anthony for helping us go deeper.

TWENTY-FOUR
Man, on the Sidewalk!

Anthony continued to expose his girls to what he described as *social field trips* as a way to normalize their perception of what life for adolescents could be. So, he tried a field trip to a local lake. The strangeness of the situation of former street girls going swimming in a local lake was further magnified as his girls frolicked like young children, while nearby mothers and their young children played alongside the Clark Academy girls. Anthony stood on the shore while his girls in their boxer shorts and tank tops stood as close to the shore as safely possible. When Anthony asked Tina if she had the swimming skills to swim out to a raft located in the center of the lake, she let out a loud laugh that insinuated that one, she did not know how to swim and two, if she actually tried, she would probably drown!

Although the Clark Academy contingent stayed for about two hours, the girls rarely ventured out from where the young children played. The more Anthony observed his girls playing in the children's restricted area, the more he realized that it was time the girls learned how to swim.

Some years ago, he witnessed three young African American boys, no older than eight or nine, being pulled out of a large flooded hole. The hole had filled up with water from the previous night's rain, which made it extremely dangerous for any child who could not swim or happened to venture into the water. The three young boys had built a flimsy wooden raft to float in the excavated hole. Tragically, they did not realize that the hole was six feet deep, and not knowing how to swim, they all drowned when their raft sank. From that day's memory, Anthony vowed if he ever had the chance as a teacher, he would ensure that his students learned how to swim, no matter the age. When he returned to the academy, he immediately called the YMCA and asked if a pool and instructor would be available for swim lessons. Chester gave his blessing, but only if the girls did not fall behind in their GED studies.

The following week Anthony and the girls waited anxiously in the YMCA lobby for their swim instructor to appear. Several homeless males sat on benches and chairs observing the young and attractive girls as if they hadn't had a meal in weeks, only this meal was fourteen young females who dressed like they were from the Oakland streets. There was always a fine line when Anthony and the girls ventured out into the community, a line between sensationalism and healthy immersion into society. In this instance, they were inside the community of YMCA, so everyone was on their best behavior. However, if they were on the street, males almost always became more overt in their behavior and catcalled, calling out, "Whoa mama" or "Hey sister," or simply created obnoxious sounds that attempted to invade the girls' physical territory.

Anthony didn't hesitate to do his part to keep the girls' behavior under wraps. Nevertheless, whenever he needed to rein the girls in, his eyes would get wide and his lips would tighten, which translated to *Knock it off, or you will all get pulled up!*

The YMCA swim teacher's name was Joanie, age twenty and a student at UC. When she met the girls, she did a double-take of the girls' off-campus street uniforms. It was not so much the girls' outfits as it was their desire for swim lessons, which from Joan's perception, didn't look right.

Her first words to the girls were a curt introduction: "I look forward to being your swim instructor. Please follow me down to the locker room and pool area."

Anthony and his female contingent all followed Joanie down some spiral stairs and through several dark, narrow passageways. The closer they got to the pool, the more intense the body odors became, which prompted DJ to comment, "The place needs more than Right Guard . . . but Left Guard as well!"

On the way to the pool, they walked past the weight-lifting room, where a muscular black male was on his back attempting to press a heavily weighted barbell. When he saw the girls walk by, a panicked expression appeared on his face. Fortunately, his expression changed when he was able to lift the barbell, and then set it down with a huge thud. Next, he waved and shouted to the girls: "You girls can disturb me any time! Except you got to warn me when you are coming, cuz I might hurt myself!"

Joanie directed Anthony to the men's locker room and then escorted the girls into the women's locker room and almost immediately there was a strange energy that overtook the room. Older women in their late sixties had just finished a water aerobics class. They immediately stopped their talking when they saw the young, attractive Clark Academy girls with their shapely bodies.

One older woman commented, "I remember when I had your bodies . . . but this is what you get to look forward to even if you work out three times a week!"

The girls only smiled and tried to be courteous. The girls went about changing into their new bathing suits, which were not particularly interesting, except for DJ, who decided to change in the bathroom alone, so no one could see her naked. Moments later she appeared in her tight-fitting black swimsuit, and of course DJ moved about like a high-priced model checking out her body in front of a mirror for all to see.

"I thought I was going to look worse but this suit pulls it all in," she mused to all onlookers. "Not bad, if I say so myself."

"Yea," said Charlene. "All 400 pounds of Big Macs, Domino's Pizza, Clint's Barbecue, etc. Girl, you got stop eatin' that stuff!"

The older women remained silent, just smiling and shaking their heads, and even a few started clapping.

Once the girls had all changed into their swimsuits, Joanie led them into the pool area. Joanie was a tall, slim woman with a swimmer's body, very muscular on the top. Tina whispered, "If I had her body, I could charge a lot more on the streets, and you can take that to the bank. "

"Ladies," said Joanie seriously, "we must start from the very beginning about how to swim and always respecting the dangers of water. I must treat you like young children who have never been in water before."

Their first major action was for the girls to delicately enter the heated pool, as if they were approaching a pool filled with killer sharks. However, once the ordeal of getting into the pool was accomplished, Joanie demonstrated some stretching exercises. Next, she moved to some aerobics exercises to help the girls get acclimated to feeling comfortable in the waist-high water. Then she had them try placing their heads underwater, which for some took about fifteen minutes. Their excuses ranged from "I do not want to get my hair wet" to "I ain't goin' to do it because my hair will get all nappy." However, in time, all the girls were able to place their heads underwater. After that test, they spent another fifteen minutes learning how to kick by holding onto to the wall. The entire lesson lasted for about thirty minutes and then Joanie allowed the girls 15 minutes for play, which resulted in splashing each other or resembling what young children might do at their first swim lesson.

Throughout the swim lesson, Anthony participated as the assistant swim instructor by keeping the girls focused with their kicking, strokes, and various exercises. However, the entire swim experience was in many ways a rite of passage toward a healthy relationship with a male for the girls to see Anthony in swim trunks and the girls, of course, with their shapely bodies accentuated by their swimsuits. The entire experience broke down the walls the girls usually put up to their nakedness, but now they were just young girls in a natural, innocent experience with their intelligent and respectful male teacher.

Once the swim session was finished, Anthony went his own way and the girls theirs, until they all met in the lobby. Nonetheless, once in the main lobby, the girls could not help but notice an aerobic dance class was about to begin. The music of Prince and others blared out of a nearby dance room. Once the girls heard the music, they all gravitated to the dance class and began to gyrate to the music. The instructor saw the girls and motioned for them to join in, which they did immediately. Anthony was happy to see the girls exercising with many older women, so he encouraged the girls to join in. After about fifteen minutes, Anthony pointed to his watch, but the girls pleaded for Antony to let them stay till the end of class, to which he agreed.

On the way home, all the girls talked about was swim class and the aerobics class, especially the music and getting to dance and exercise at the same time.

"Maybe we can have a swim lesson and then after go to the dance class," suggested Jewels.

"Yeah," agreed DJ. "I think I lost about fifteen pounds already!"

When they returned to school, Anthony met with Chester and asked if he could sign the girls up for aerobics class.

'Well, I will do anything that will lower their hormones," he replied, "except, what will it cost?"

"The instructor said she would give us a 50 percent reduction because we are a local school," responded Anthony, to Chester's delight.

Thus began the aerobics class as well as the swim class.

The girls attended two swim and aerobic classes, but by the third aerobics class, something unusual began to appear on the street outside the YMCA. The aerobics class was in a dance room that ushered in the outside street, and with its large windows, it was a perfect advertisement for exercise to the entire world. The only problem was that outside was a large contingency of homeless people, mostly men, who would congregate in and around YMCA for free showers and use of the bathrooms.

Word on the streets spread quickly about the young, beautiful girls who participated in the Monday 4 p.m. YMCA aerobics class. This attraction was accentuated by the young, shapely teens who danced their painful hearts out in the class. In fact, the class became one of the biggest draws on the Berkeley street scene! By the fourth class, the crowd of males had grown to such a degree that many males were now blocking the sidewalks and bodies began to spill out into the street. What's more, one enterprising individual roped off a part of the sidewalk, added a few chairs, and began exchanging cigarettes for a closer view! When a few onlookers began pushing and shoving and trying to tear down the rope, a mob of homeless males began to create a major riot, until the police were called in and quelled the anger. Ultimately, the girls and the aerobics class had to be canceled, much to the girls' sadness, although swim classes were always a positive experience.

JEWELS ODOM COMMENTARY #41

It seems that Anthony figured out how to get us in touch with our abusive pasts. Such trips to Lake Anza and swimming with young children as well as additional trips to petting zoos seem to support our childhood needs.

TWENTY-FIVE
Andrea

Anthony was leading the girls in PE class, doing jumping-jack exercises. When DJ attempted jumping jacks, she only moved her arms up and down lazily, like Big Bird from *Sesame Street* fame.

"If you are goin' to play Big Bird, you need to put more life into it," hassled Tina, flapping her arms like some ostrich.

Anthony turned to the rest of the girls and directed everyone to cool down, except for DJ, who needed to warm up and work out.

"DJ owes me and the class fifteen real jumping jacks," ordered Anthony.

"This is as real as it gets!" she said, flapping her arms. "What you see is what you got. Remember, I got to deal with more gravity than the rest of you lightweights!"

DJ started counting her jumping jacks. "One . . . three . . . five . . . seven . . . nine . . . eleven . . . thirteen . . . fifteen! Well, you did not say how I should count. This is called not getting even!"

Finally, she fell on the floor, breathless.

Anthony took out a slip of paper and began to read to the girls.

"We have been invited to enter a relay team in this year's High School City Cup," He eyed the girls with a very concerned look, expecting he would not get any takers. "I need four volunteers."

The girls continued to cool down by lying on the floor and generally ignored Anthony's announcement.

"What is the problem?" he asked, concerned. "Our school needs four volunteers to compete in the City Cup. It would be good for the school to

151

get some positive publicity; plus it would look good on your resumes to say that you competed in the city event with other schools."

Jewels eyed Anthony and nodded her head tentatively.

"Okay," Jewels explained, "we can get some experience running, something that is legal and I do not mean drug-running."

"That makes one!" said Anthony enthusiastically. "We need three more or it ain't going to happen."

"I worked as a look out for my homeboys and I did a lot of running then," offered Angel. "I guess I'm in."

"So that makes you Speedy Gonzalez?" asked DJ.

"Do not ever cap on me, girl," said Angel. "And when was the last time you moved anything in your body with speed, and I don't mean your mouth with fast food!"

"I will ignore you on the grounds that I will seriously sit on you!" returned DJ, smiling and showing off her overstated gold tooth in the front of her mouth.

DJ stood up and started walking toward Angel. Then Angel, who was half DJ's size, stood up and started walking backward, away from DJ.

"I was just goin' to give Angel a big hug," said DJ with a sarcastic smile.

Angel just mumbled something in Spanish.

"Enough of this ghetto education stuff," said Anthony. "I got two, so who will be the third? I will even take you to Clint's even if we compete and come in last."

"I'm not running unless we win," exclaimed Angel. "I am not going to let some yuppie, nerd, valley girl, white honkie bitch beat me or us!"

Finally, Patricia and DJ raised their hands simultaneously.

Over on the side, standing alone, Andrea raised her hand slightly, the girl who rarely if ever socialized or engaged with the girls.

"Aaahhhhh, are you really sayin' you want in?" asked Anthony, surprised at Andrea's response.

"I think maybe she is just exercising her arm," responded Kim.

JEWELS ODOM COMMENTARY #42

Andrea's abuse or abandonment was different from that of most girls. Ours was more physical or in your face, abuse that came early in life, and then there was foster care, residential treatment, and the streets. For her, at least she knows her

father and maybe even her mother, who she never mentions, but we all know that
her pain is different and something we cannot relate to. And when she raises her
hand to participate in the relay, we are stunned by her desire to race, but also it is
her way of reaching out and becoming a part of the group.

"So, you are saying that you want to be on the relay team?" asked Patricia directly.

"Don't push her," intervened Jewels. "Maybe she was just thinking about it."

"Are you sure?" asked roommate Patricia. "You can change your mind."

Andrea nodded her head.

"Alright!" yelled Patricia. "Andrea wants to run, so let her run!"

Andrea flashed a brief smile like she was being liberated from her past.

"Okay, we got our four," said Patricia, looking at DJ. "Were you raising your hand because you want to run to the bathroom and take a dump?"

Kim laughed so hard that she fell to the floor, "That is cold! DJ wants to run to the bathroom and take a dump!"

"Well, maybe I did and maybe I didn't, but he did say four runners," said DJ coyly.

"Seriously?" asked Patricia. "They only allow four in the relay. If you join that would mean five, because you are really two people in one. Anyhow, how you going to be in some mother-effiin' relay race when you can barely make it up the stairs to your bedroom at night? All this is pussy talk, when we all know she needs to lose weight or she is going to have a freakin' heart attack someday! I will tell you . . . I am through with funerals. If any of you OD or get shot because you are showing colors, it's your problem! And DJ, this is real! If you don't go on a diet, you will end up dead! And you can take that to the bank, graveyard, or wherever your big booty fits, which ain't goin to be in some freakin' coffin. I cannot handle any more deaths!"

"She didn't hear a word you said," remarked Kim. "We don't like callin' you on your shit, but nothing else is working!"

Anthony remained quiet, letting each one wolf or have their say.

DJ let them have their say and then said, "I hate to break up this meeting called 'pick on DJ,' but I think it's snack time."

"I got one last thing to say and it is about Anthony," said Patricia. "I mean we got all this stuff to do and now we got to train for the race, and what Anthony wants, Anthony gets, but now it is payback time. I want to make a deal. If we compete, you got to let us dress you up for the end-of-the-year dinner, and we get to choose the restaurant, and it ain't goin to be Clint's, but a real restaurant where you have to get all dressed up and stuff.

"Okay," said Anthony, hesitating, "but you have to compete . . . no quitting at the last minute!"

"Alright, you're on!" Patricia announced. "Everybody, let's put our hands together to show that we all agree."

The girls and Anthony all put their hands together.

"I was thinking," offered DJ. "For a kicker, if we don't finish last, you also have to take us to Clint's Barbecue."

"She doesn't give up!" screamed Patricia. "In one ear and out the next or in her mouth and out the you-know-where!"

JEWELS ODOM COMMENTARY #43

I put these statistics under DJ's pillow to read. For kids and adolescents ages two to nineteen: the percent of obesity was 18.5 percent or about 13.5 million, and about 14 percent of two- to five-year-olds, about 18.5 percent among six- to eleven-year-olds and 20.5 percent among twelve- to nineteen-year-olds.

Andrea, Patricia, Angel, and Jewels each carried a wooden baton while they ran through the Oakland streets to Lake Meritt, an inner-city lake located within the confines of downtown Oakland. Anthony followed close behind in his Saab station wagon. He held a stopwatch in his hand and periodically glanced at it to measure the girls' workout time. When they ran past a local barbershop, Cecil the barber rushed outside and yelled at the girls as they ran by.

"Whooaaaaaaa mama!" he heckled loudly. "I like your tight shorts but those tight shorts ain't going to win you no race. You got to move your arms! Dammit, ladies, move your arms!"

The girls only smiled, shook their behinds, and waved back.

The distance to Lake Meritt and back was about four miles. When they reached Lake Merritt, they would run around the lake and then back to school.

"Keep your weight forward, please!" yelled Anthony from his car window. "And like Cecil said, move your arms!"

All the girls completed the four miles and returned to school and began to cool down when Anthony appeared carrying several boxes.

"I have a surprise for you," said Anthony, presenting the girls with boxes that held New Balance running shoes. "You will not be running on the road but on a cork track, which will be different than running on pavement."

The girls tried on their new running shoes and for the next hour showed them off to anyone who happened to come their way and then some. The rest of the girls became upset because they didn't get new running shoes, so of course Anthony had to buy ten more pairs of running shoes for the rest of the girls. Chester footed half the bill, and the staff, including Anthony, paid for the rest. The best part about the new shoes was that the girls refused to take them off! They wore them when they attended school, when they danced, on field trips, and even when Anthony took them out for frozen yogurt.

The running shoes served two purposes: First, the girls stopped wearing their high heels, and second, they were advertising to the world that they were exercising, although he was still waiting for the rest of the girls to get into jogging.

Anthony was able to talk to Clint's Barbecue's owner and then a local sports store that was willing to give them 50 percent off on fourteen running suits with the name "Clint's Barbecue" printed on the back. Printed on the front was "The Clark Academy." The next time they went out for frozen yogurt, *all* the girls wore their running outfits, which created a sense of teamwork among the girls and for their school.

Also, when the girls raced upstairs and downstairs, there was no longer the loud persistent gunfire of noise, but only quiet footsteps, thanks to their New Balance running shoes. In fact, whenever they went off school property, their running outfits were now a normal dress code, which according to Chester and the rest of the staff, was nothing short of a miracle.

"You keep taking us out for frozen yogurt, and I will keep wearing my warm-up suit," said DJ, who had to have her suit special-ordered as a triple large.

And there was Andrea, with her black tattoos on her hands and arms and the dark shadows under her eyes and her long black hair hiding her face that made her look like someone out of the TV show *The Munster's*. Now, Andrea, who barely spoke and always looked away or down when spoken to, had gone through a transformation since she volunteered to run on the relay team. At first the girls were skeptical that she could actually run ten yards; however, when they went out for their first jog, Andrea stunned all the girls by her speed and endurance.

"I do not know if it was the running outfit or the track shoes, but something came over this girl," said DJ. "She went from gothic queen to jogger queen. And she even said hello to me and made eye contact. Whatever she is eating, maybe she can share it with me!"

JEWELS ODOM COMMENTARY #44

Anthony has failed for many months to change the girls' ghetto heads as to how they dress. I feel it is mostly mistrust for the Man on the Floor. The girls are not willing to give up their street identity to just any man, even Anthony, who they trust. He was patient, regardless of the number of times the girls used their high heels to stomp angrily up the stairs, or when he took us on field trips and the girls played their stupid dress-up Halloween street games. Now that we are working out, Chester doesn't get into any of his control-freak moods, but lets the girls have their say about how they dress in public. If he had forced the girls into changing their so-called street garb, he would have had a rebellion and maybe even a few runners. With our new running outfits and shoes, Anthony has given the girls the chance to choose a new identity that is healthier. And the outside world looks at us differently too. In my opinion, it is a win-win for all of us!

TWENTY-SIX

To Be a Snitch or Not to Be a Snitch!

JEWELS ODOM COMMENTARY #45

School meetings would bring out little territorial spots in our study hall room. Our so-called spot or turf was claimed at our first school meeting, and no one—I mean no one—would take someone's spot for fear of losing her life! My spot is over in a corner on the floor and gives me space to daydream, but I still have a view of all that is going on, inside and outside. Others want windowsills because it allows them to look out of the windows when things get particularly boring. They like to observe an occasional pedestrian moving on the sidewalk in front of the school and, if really bored, watch Mrs. Jackson on her daily walk with Louis. Ex-gang-bangers usually choose spots nearest doors for a quick escape, and hoes like to be out in front, trying to be in control like a quick sale on the streets.

Finally, our turf needs don't stop in the study hall room but carry over to the classroom, on the school bus, at the dinner table, and so on. I guess one's space was always connected to survival on the streets.

"Ok Mr. Job-Finder," DJ said, "how much money do we get for working?"

"You will be working for free but getting training in a vocational interest of your choice," returned Anthony, looking over at Chester for support.

"I thought slavery went out with Lincoln," DJ countered. "I know you are goin' to get a kickback. Am I right or am I right?"

"No kickbacks," interrupted Chester. "Just the experience of working is the kickback and it will look good on your resume when you leave here and study nuclear physics at Stanford or Harvard."

DJ just shook her head and said, "Still slave labor!"

After a few weeks of phone calls to different schools, rest homes, and so forth, Anthony found jobs for DJ, Tina, and Jewels.

DJ would begin working as a candy-striper at a local hospital. When the students saw DJ in her red, white, and blue candy-striper uniform, they couldn't resist calling her "Peppermint Patty," (but under their breath you know they wanted to call her Peppermint Fatty) to which DJ replied, "I sort of like having my job connected to candy."

Tina would begin working in the public library stacking books.

"It's not a bad job, except a few homeboys ended up in the library and when they saw me working there, they wanted more than books. I could handle them, but it was all the old homeless dudes who came in to use the bathroom and of course the nerds who were definitely not my style."

When Jewels heard of the program, she connected with a job at a local Montessori school. Anthony gave her an article about Montessori's philosophy.

"You don't have to be nervous," said Anthony to Jewels as he drove her to the local Montessori school. Although Jewels would be working as an aide for only a few hours one day a week, it could be a positive experience since she was interested in becoming a teacher.

"Working with kids," Anthony explained, "gives you a feeling of unconditional love, which is something that could be healing considering your difficult past."

"So, that's why you became a teacher director at our school for crazies?" she asked jokingly. "This school would be the last place you would get unconditional love from us girls! I know this sounds like I am tripping," she continued, "but someday I would like to be a Montessori teacher. I never told anyone except Mrs. Jackson, but I think I could be a good teacher because of all the bad school experiences I had. Also, I used to help the little kids with homework when I lived in residential treatment. You learn quickly about the good, the bad, and the ugly when you are helping them with their homework."

JEWELS ODOM COMMENTARY #46

When I was eight years old, I attended a school that was close to some Oakland projects. More than once, a dead body was found on our school playground, because of a gang shooting or a druggie who OD'd on bad drugs. Imagine what it was like for an eight-year-old kid to start school, while a dead body was being dragged from your playground! Police cars, ambulances, and crowds of onlookers only made a bad situation worse! I mean we were quickly sent back to our classrooms, but for the remainder of the day, all you could think about was the dead body and worry that maybe the next time it could be you.

And then there was this warning bell that would signal us to duck under our desks, because of gang wars or when drug dealers and the cops would be shooting it out right in front of our school! My classroom still showed the scars of bullet wounds in its walls! Go visit Washington School on East 14th Street and check out classroom number 3, which faces the street. Look nearest the wall, along the side windows and you will see two or three bullet holes. Hello!

Also, our walking fieldtrips down East 14th Street to the local library never lacked danger. More than once, our field trip was interrupted by police cars speeding up and down East 14th Street, traveling about 100 miles an hour, chasing drug dealers and gang bangers and so forth. It was amazing how our teachers always reacted like nothing was happening. They would quickly move us back to the school grounds, wait until the danger was over, and proceed to the library. Such was the unpredictable and dangerous lives of the eight hundred or so kids who attended my elementary school in the hood.

"Did you read the article about Montessori I gave you?" asked Anthony. "It would help you to have a better understanding about working with preschoolers, particularly orphaned or abandoned kids."

"Yeah," Jewels said, "I connected with the article right way because I have felt like an orphan most of my life. I had to make it on my own, so maybe that would make me sort of an expert when it comes to understanding kids who have been abandoned by their parents. When you are abandoned, you don't trust. Do you know I still do not trust anyone at our school, not even you, Anthony? I went to the streets because of all the sexual abuse I experienced in foster care and residential treatment programs. I did not trust the system."

They drove into the parking lot of the school and noticed the kids were outside playing on the playground while younger children were actively involved in a sandbox pouring water into cups and so forth. A teacher stood off to the side simply letting the kids play in an undisturbed way.

"See what I mean!" said Jewels excitedly. "Montessori said that kids need freedom to learn without adults always bothering them. I think I am going to like working here."

"I think you may be right. I'll pick you up at 5 p.m."

"*Arrivederci*," she said, getting out of the car. "It means 'good-bye' in Italian. I'm even thinking of taking an Italian class at the JC when I leave Clark."

"*Ciao*," returned Antony. "It means 'hello' and now 'good-bye' in Italian. Enjoy your day."

JEWELS ODOM COMMENTARY #47

I read that Montessori created her school for orphans who all had attachment disorders, which means they lacked trust, which is something us girls deal with all the time. To teach her orphans how to read, she gave them sandpaper letters to learn the alphabet. I mean they could drag their fingers over the sandpaper letters as they said the alphabet . . . something about the part of the brain that made you trust and learn better? One last thing that I learned about her was that she was the first woman doctor in Italy. I think she was very cool!

TWENTY-SEVEN
Track Meet!

The week before the track meet, Anthony and the girls finally had the chance to train for the 4-by-400-yard relay race on a local high school cork track. Each runner would be responsible for her 100-yard segment. On this day, Anthony prepared the girls for the relay and the passing of baton by giving an egg to Angel, who would start the 400-yard race.

Angel gave Anthony a sly look and smiled, "Not bad, *amigo*! You want us to use an egg instead of a baton to make sure we make the right pass to each other. Very smart!"

"There is reason for each student's particular place on the team," explained Anthony. "I want Angel to run first because she has excellent reaction time, which means that she will get off to a fast start at the beginning of the race. Andrea will run second because she needs a running start to be successful. Patrician runs third because she has good hands and will present a good pass to Jewels, our fastest runner. If we are at all close to the leaders, or even behind, Jewels is fast enough to catch and run past the leaders."

After the workout, Anthony had all the girls watch a segment of the movie *Ben Hur*.

"I am just going to show you one part of *Ben Hur* that might help you understand about teamwork in a relay race."

He wanted to show them a part of the movie that described the famous chariot race and how each horse played a critical role to win the race.

"Although they ran as one," he explained, "each horse played an important role in the chariot race. The consistent steady one on the inside was not the fastest horse, but he would keep the other three horses in line and so forth. There was a reason why or where each horse's role existed in the race."

JEWELS ODOM COMMENTARY #48

Anthony often shows films to make a point. Anthony always said, "The visual reinforces the audio to support the story line. . . so, what better way to make a point?"

One day after track practice, he showed a very intense movie called Gallipoli *to teach us that running was not simply physical but also the relationships you develop with other runners.*

Gallipoli was about two young Australian runners who met at a track competition and decided to join the Australian army to fight the Turks in a place called Gallipoli.

Because the boys were excellent runners, they were selected as runners to deliver the orders or messages to officers on the front lines. But only one of the boys was selected to be a runner and his friend was moved to a regiment that would be sent over the top to face the Turks' machine guns.

Time after time, regiments were sent over the top and massacred by the Turks. After many failed attacks, the British commander gave in and called off the next attack. But our runner must deliver the message to his friend's regiment before they might go over the top and face deadly machine gun fire. We follow the young runner racing through rows of solders about to go over the top, but just as he delivers the message to the commanding officer to stop the attack, his friend's regiment is sent over the top and he sees his friend killed by machine gun fire.

After we watched the movie, most of us broke down and cried. For many of us, it was really the first time we ever cried at school or in front of each other. The lesson Anthony was trying to teach us was that it is okay to show our true emotions and that if we cried or showed tears, it would not mean we were weak but actually that we trusted the group.

The girls had spent most of the week nervously thinking about the district-wide track meet. Only Jewels tried to calm the girls' nerves, which could break out anytime, and then it could be ugly until you had to separate the girls from killing each other.

"It's not going to be any big deal," repeated Jewels to the other three girls. "You run and then in minutes it is all over and we get to go home and party!"

"Easy for you to say," returned Patricia, the Clark Academy's first runner. "If I don't get out fast, well, you will be running behind. So don't sugarcoat the meet. It's probably the biggest thing that ever happened to our school. Well, not really. Maybe DJ getting dressed up like a big peppermint fatty."

She looked around quickly to see if DJ was around. Fortunately, DJ had on ear plugs and was getting in her required exercise routine moving around to Michel Jackson's *Thriller* album, one of her favorites.

Finally, the day arrived and to the girls' surprise the track meet was a lot bigger a spectacle then they anticipated.

The stands were full of spectators, each school's cheering section complete with banners and cheerleaders from the different participating schools. The Clark Academy girls and staff made signs and rang bells to let the girls know they were in full support of "the team that nobody knows!"

Jewels, Andrea, Angel, and Patricia were all lying on the grass silently waiting to be called for the final heat of the 4-by-400 relay.

Anthony stood with the girls, trying to emit a sense of calmness. However, the pressure of the final race was taking a toll on the girls, as there was little or no interaction among them; they refused to talk or make eye contact with each other. It was what you might expect from street kids running against girls who could never venture into the world of the Clark Academy girls. Also, our girls were running against girls who knew they had a future, which would mean college and beyond. The Clark Academy girls' lives had been programmed with unpredictability since the beginning of their lives, and as such, predictability was something these girls may never know.

Any sense of pride or allegiance from each other came from their new blue sweatsuits with "The Clark Academy" printed on the front and "Clint's Barbecue" on the back, thanks to the owner of Clint's, who proudly sat alone in the stands.

Andrea kept looking over at the grandstands, hoping her father would show. She'd asked Anthony to call the military base and let him know that she was running in the 4-by-400 relay and it would mean a great deal if he came.

Anthony had left a message on his answering machine and the father had yet to get back to him.

"Don't worry," said Patricia. "He will be here."

Andrea remained quiet, but her eyes were fixated on the grandstand.

JEWELS ODOM COMMENTARY #49

Now Andrea even raises her hand in class discussions, expressing her opinions on all topics; even on weekends, she accompanies us on outings in the hood. The greatest transformation occurred at the UC pottery class, where she met a boy who asked her out on a movie date . . . of course, that's if Chester approves of the young man.

Brother Chi walked over to where the girls were stretching and only nodded and smiled in approval.

"What words of wisdom do you have for us before we go into battle, oh Great One?" Angel asked, without stopping her stretching routine.

"No words, just have fun and enjoy the moment," he said in his usual soft voice. "And yes, to run like cheetah, you must become the cheetah."

"Ladies, the 400-yard relay race will begin in fifteen minutes," the announcer's voice boomed out over the loudspeaker.

"Jewels," said Anthony, "it might be a good idea if you stretched a bit. Remember, that hamstring can tighten up."

Jewels was lying on the grass. She opened her eyes and gave Anthony a sarcastic smile but made no comment.

"When I'm nervous I need a smoke something fierce," remarked Patricia. "Anyone got a smoke? Just joking!"

Anthony took out Jewels's new track shoes, which she had resisted wearing, and said pointedly to Jewels, "These are yours. You left them at the school."

"I told you before," responded Jewels curtly, "I like my old wheels to be comfortable, so I will go with what got me here."

"This is a corked track and the traction will be different from the experience of running on the streets or at Lake Merritt," returned Anthony.

"No way!" responded Jewels. "I want to think I am running on the streets and not some funky cork track. I want to run like Chi said . . . run like Cheetah . . . you got to be cheetah. And to survive on the streets, you got to run like a cheetah. I like to keep the same feeling with my wheels."

Anthony just shook his head, remained silent, and placed her shoes next to her.

"Well," he said, walking away, "I respect your opinion but again this is a different track."

"I read about this African runner who ran a marathon in the Olympics barefoot through the streets of Rome," Jewels defended to the rest of the girls. "They were not going to let him run but he convinced the powers-that-be that he would be alright and they let him run and guess what? He won a gold medal . . . so there!"

Angel scanned the crowd and saw the Clark School girls and staff sitting in the bleachers. She spied DJ and Angel rubbed her hands over her breasts and threw DJ a big kiss. In response, DJ turned around and stuck her behind out and shook it to no end, causing Angel to fall on the ground laughing.

Sitting next to Toni and Chester was Mrs. Jackson, who had a look of confusion until Toni pointed out Jewels.

"These days I don't see too well," said Mrs. Jackson, squinting, "but now I see Jewels. Yep, like I always said, she's got a runner's body."

"Remember," said Anthony, "this is it . . . the final heat. There are no other heats. Do not hold back anything. You will make us all proud by your performance today, so don't worry about winning or losing. Be aggressive and stay in your lane. Keep your weight forward, move your arms, and make your pass smooth—just like we practiced—and breathe when you're feeling tense. Angel will give the baton to Andrea like she's passing her the egg, firmly but delicately. Andrea will give the baton to Patricia, who will then pass the baton to Jewels. Remember the receiver of the baton makes her break when she feels the distance is about right or just how we practiced. It is all about timing, and then Jewels will be able to do what she does best . . . turn on the afterburners."

A long black suburban pulled in and parked. Climbing out of the car and heading for the stands in all his gold jewelry and fine threads was Latrel. He swaggered up the grandstand stairs and made eye contact with Chester and Toni.

"What does Mr. Slime Ball want?" asked Toni with a look of disgust.

"What they all want," said Chester, "to be seen by the girls. Like, I am a normal slime ball!"

The girls all moved to their positions when the public address speaker notified the runners that it would be the final announcement for the 4-by-400 relay.

Latrell gave Chester and Toni a cold stare and looked off to the track.

A tall black girl appeared in the lane next to Patricia.

"I don't think I have seen you before," she said, sizing up Patricia in the next lane. "Hey, great uni's, especially Clint's Barbecue . . . best ribs around!"

"No, I'm new to this game," returned Patricia. "Most of my running has been from blue or black!"

The girl looked at Patricia, not knowing if she was serious or not, and only laughed. "Very funny. Yeah! Go Clint's!"

"If we win we get free barbecue," said Patricia. "Oh yeah!"

"Damn," she returned, "wish we had that incentive. Anyhow, good luck."

Yeah," returned Patricia. "The same to you. Good luck and do not slip on any banana peels. Oh, one last thing," she added. "Tell me who's hot in this race . . . I mean who is the serious comp?"

"Well, I would like to say our team, but according to coach, the team in lane number 3 is quick at the start and the girl in lane 6 to your right ran a fast 100 in her last meet."

"Five minutes to race time," announced the starter. "Please go to your positions. Patricia suddenly realized that she had to pee. "Aaahhhhhhh hello, sir?" she addressed an official standing off to the side. "Where is the nearest potty?"

The official looked confused and then said, "I am not sure if you got time, miss, but over there behind the stands is a bathroom."

"Thank you," said Patricia rushing to the bathroom, while a few of the runners glanced in her direction and only shook their heads. Anthony looked up from his program and did not see Patricia on the track and thought she had bolted to have a cigarette.

"Damn it!" he said to himself, "I should not have left her alone! She is taking a smoke!"

"Please clear the track for the final heat of the 4-by-400-yard relay," repeated the public-address speaker. "Please clear the track!"

Patricia squatted down under the bleachers and began peeing.

Angel made the sign of the cross and Jewels began to stretch in her lane. Andrea stretched, and then ran in place. The runners were all in their starting places.

"Runners, take your position," announced the starter. There was a slight pause of about five seconds and then the starter's gun went off and the runners all shot out from their respective places.

At the crack of the gun, Patricia rushed over to join her place on the track and waited for Angel to pass the baton to Andrea. Angel got off to a slow start and was about five yards behind and running next to last in seventh place; however, at the very end of her sprint, she made up ground and was only ten yards behind the runner who was running in third place. Angel's pass to Andrea was smooth and to everyone's surprise, Andrea not only held her own, but moved the Clark team to third place when she passed the baton to Patricia. Now, the Clark Academy girls were in second place, but still about ten yards behind the leader.

Over in the stands the Clark Academy girls and staff were standing and screaming, urging their team on. Over on the side was Andrea's father, who had appeared just in time for the start of the race. He stood off to the side, looking serious with a straight face. Three-fourths of the way through the race, Patricia attempted to make a final pass to Jewels, but Patricia hesitated, and Jewels had to slow down, which caused Jewels to trip slightly and moved the Clark Academy back to third place. Jewels righted herself and hit her stride and was clearly the fastest runner in the final lap, but then she stumbled slightly, which allowed for three runners to pass her, which caused her to finish seventh or next to last. Disgusted, Jewels threw the baton down angrily and did not stop running until she was off the track and onto the Oakland streets. Jewels found a quiet street and sat down on a side street curb and buried her face in her hands and sobbed.

Anthony ran from the track meet looking for Jewels but gave up and returned to the girls, who were distraught about losing the event.

"Miss Know-It-All and her stupid wheels," complained Patricia. "She should have listened to Anthony and worn the right running shoes. We could have won the race if it were not for her. She screwed Bonita and got her to give up her kids and look what happened to Bonita. Now she screwed us . . . all that training for nothing."

"She did her best," returned Anthony. "She did not trip on purpose. Bury the hatchet. This meet was a good experience, so we need to move on. We got the GED test tomorrow, which is more important. Let's go back to the school, have a good dinner, maybe watch a movie, get a good night's sleep, and take the GED."

"Easy for you to say," interrupted Patricia. "I don't care if I ever see her again!"

Andrea and Angel remained silent as they walked over to the Clark Academy contingency, who were all trying to appear upbeat.

"Well, you girls did great!" said Chester. "If Jewels had not stumbled by accident you might have won."

Toni appeared with Mrs. Jackson and they gave the girls hugs.

"I am so proud of you girls," said Toni. "We almost won . . . the school that nobody knows about almost won! I am so proud of all of you. Now we need to find Jewels. Where's Jewels?"

Chester looked over at Toni and said, "Jewels decided to walk home. She was a little upset and needed to be alone."

"Maybe she should keep walking," said Patricia.

Toni gave Patricia a stern look.

Anthony explained, "Maybe, she just needs to walk it off."

Mrs. Jackson sounded worried, "But that is not like Jewels to leave and not say goodbye."

Andrea stood quietly, searching the stands for her dad until he appeared, walking slowly over to her. She stood for a moment, not knowing how to respond, and then she ran to him and they embraced. Andrea started crying, "I . . . I didn't think you would ever come!

The colonel didn't say anything until Anthony appeared and said, "She ran a great race."

"Yes," said the father, looking at Andrea. "I couldn't have been prouder. I only wish your mother were alive to see you run."

The girls all boarded their beat-up school bus and returned to school. On the journey back to school, all the girls stayed quiet until DJ said, "Let it go, you guys. I mean you girls did great. It wasn't Jewels's fault. It was an accident. Let it freakin' go." DJ paused momentarily and said jubilantly, "I think we should celebrate and all go to Clints?"

No one responded to DJ's short speech. They just stared out of the bus windows, each with their own thoughts about the day.

JEWELS ODOM COMMENTARY #50

Yes, I screwed up big time! It wasn't so much losing the race but it was failing the girls when someone they needed to rely on let them down. It may seem like it was only a race that we lost but it was a lot more. We were on this stage that said we belonged with all those large schools that had all this respect. Then comes the Clark Academy with the words Clint's Barbecue printed on the back of our jerseys. It was the first time in our lives that maybe, just maybe, people would respect us and I threw it all out the window. Our one time we could get respect and think that we belonged.

TWENTY-EIGHT
Top Dog or Shop Bully

Since Anthony assumed the position as the Clark Academy school director, his relationship with Madison, his girlfriend, could be described as being more on a downward spiral than an upward one. He would return each day from teaching and/or his director's position emotionally drained and burned out! To compound the school stress, he was becoming more distant with Madison, due in part to their financial disparities. That is, Madison's life could be described as almost idyllic. Along with her art therapist practice, she was an excellent artist, possessed a PhD in geology, was a published author on cross-country skiing, and was a competitive cross-country skier! In addition, she possessed zero school loans and owned a beautiful home in the Berkeley hills.

Bottom line—she was financially independent due to a large inheritance from her grandfather. However, Anthony still had student loans to pay and the financial living arrangement was 50/50, which also placed stress on their relationship because Madison liked to travel to far-off places for vacations. In the world of 50/50 financial relationships, Anthony almost always found himself behind the eight ball, trying to maintain the relationship while dealing with extraneous financial pressures due in part to his relationship with Madison, although she suggested they negotiate or reduce the 50/50 financial relationship, but Anthony always resisted as a matter of pride.

The longer he worked at the school, the more he felt that she couldn't understand the pressure that he had. The pressure of failure was a constant reminder that if he did fail, the girls could end up back on the streets or at CYA, and their perception of life would be changed dramatically from hopes and dreams to one of possible rape and abuse in prison.

They had discussions about his stress and the school's disorganization and how Chester and Toni unconsciously found ways to disrupt his school program. From Toni being late for counseling sessions to Chester always concerned about the bottom line of money, they only made Anthony's job more stressful.

As the school year went on, the distance between Anthony and Madison increased until finally she suggested he find an apartment, yet "still see each other on weekends."

Further, although she only conducted two art therapy sessions at the school, the girls always asked about Madison and wondered why she never came back, which in Anthony's mind only gave them a feeling of rejection associated with the girl's serious abandonment issues.

And on more than one occasion, the girls voiced their anger toward Madison about starting and stopping her sessions, particularly now that they had opened up emotionally to her. Although Toni was an admirable replacement, she was no Madison and the girls didn't mince words when it came to expressing their feelings.

"What the hell is that about?" complained Patricia. "I don't show my stuff to just nobody! I trusted her and she gets up and splits on us. It's bullshit!"

Although Anthony tried to encourage Madison to come and do more sessions, her anger toward Anthony and the school only made her more distant toward him, which was rapidly putting an end to the relationship.

"I do not think it would be fair to the girls if I continued to conduct sessions while our relationship is on hold due to the stress the school is causing," she explained.

"Maybe when things settle down between us, I can come in again. Sorry, but this is how I feel."

JEWELS ODOM COMMENTARY #51

We all know is that Anthony and Madison's relationship is on the outs because whenever we ask about her, Anthony only gives a short "okay," which, in our minds, is really all he has to say. However, when it comes to relationships in general, Toni and Chester's relationship is light years away from Anthony's. The "Heckle and Jeckle duo," as we've come to call Chester and Toni, always seem to be on the same page, although they often play their little verbal games simply to keep us off-balance. When Toni says one thing, Chester almost always takes the opposite view, as if to teach us that there are two sides to every idea and argument. Also, Toni is strong enough to go nose-to-nose with him, which shows us how to handle the Man on the Floor and to never back down from what you truly believe in. In my opinion, they are perfectly suited to have a school for street girls who are very street smart and who can push the envelope, but only so far. Chester or Toni will eventually jump in and move us in the right direction.

Finally, in the world of relationships, we all know that they are having more fun than we are, which is an indication of how strong their relationship is and a good example for other staff and their relationships, including the girls, who, for the most part, have never had the opportunity to be up close to a happy marriage. Rather than getting angry, Chester and Toni often find a way to see the lightness in any obstacle and can move on to more important issues; obviously, that is always difficult for us girls.

JEWELS ODOM COMMENTARY #52

When Anthony finally said he had moved out of his house with Madison, we could see the pain in his face. It was amazing how the girls changed from being pissed off or only on their "me, me" trip and became almost motherly to Anthony. So, for a few days, the girls were real nice and didn't hassle Anthony, but that only lasted a few days and then we all returned to our normal "me first" selves. Anthony knew something was up when DJ didn't constantly barter for food for an entire week or that Patricia didn't have a meltdown for no reason at all.

And to make matters worse for Anthony, one afternoon when I passed by Anthony's office, I heard Chester ask him point blank why he didn't want to be his friend. They both had attended Harvard and all, but it was really the first time I felt sorry for Chester or, for that matter, Anthony. Here were two educated guys, one black and one white, working with a bunch of crazies, and one was reaching out to be friends? It wasn't racism on Anthony's part, but you could see he had too much on his plate and he could not take on another relationship. Still, I know what Mrs. T. would say to the two of them: "And you can take that to Dr. Joyce Brothers for all I care."

One last thing. There is Jamie, who came over from the Queen Street School to help Anthony out and work with us with the GED test. Jamie is petite and very attractive, but hard as nails when dealing with us girls. At first, we played *our little intimidation games to see what she was made of, which lasted about two seconds.*

"Don't play your little street games with me!" she said loudly to Patricia on her first day. Patricia was always the first to test a newcomer. "I will pull your ass up before you know it and send you back to the hall without blinking an eye. You are here to pass the GED. If you can't follow the rules, there are other girls at the hall who can take your place!

Jamie quickly got her point across and the girls never gave her any real trouble. Sure, they would moan and complain or "play the dozens" about school-work, but that was about it.

One other thing we noticed was how Jamie and Anthony looked at each other when things were going well. It was like they felt this deep connection, both being on the same page. Some of the girls set up a little contest as to when things would get romantic with the two. The winner would get a free meal at Clint's Barbecue.

Still, relationships with staff are a "no no" for the obvious reason that if two staff members got too close and then it fell apart, the vibe on the floor would change from good to really bad. I mean when working on the floor with us girls, you have to be "on" all the time. You can't be on some head trip because of a bad relationship. The problem for staff was the job could be a major burnout and it was easy to look for ways to fill that up by having a so-called intimate relationship.

TWENTY-NINE

Can't Always Run Away from Failure!

Anthony sat on Chester's so-called "sucking couch," while Toni and Chester sat behind Chester's desk. Anthony had this worried expression on his face as he listened carefully to Chester, who was on the phone talking to the police.

"This is Chester Barkley, executive director of the Clark Academy. I want to report a missing person. Yes . . . around 3:30 p.m. . . . near Mayor's Stadium. Tall black girl . . . 18 years old . . . dressed in a blue track outfit. Her name is Jewels Odom. Yes . . . she is a student at the Clark Academy."

"Oh yeah," replied the officer, "we all know Miss Odom. If we find her, we will pick her up and bring her back to your school."

"I hope you find her because she has this very important test she needs to take tomorrow," said Chester.

Chester hung up and looked at Anthony. "It's her decision."

"Yes, but that is not the problem," returned Anthony, concerned. "It's the rest of the girls who are scheduled to take it. Jewels is their leader. She tutors the girls and gives them their self-confidence. If she is not there, the rest of the girls' confidence could be affected. I do not want to put it off. They are ready to take the test now."

"Let's keep our fingers crossed that she will show up," answered Chester.

JEWELS ODOM COMMENTARY #53

I felt I had let the girls down in the track meet. I ran away instead of facing failure, but as I look back at what we achieved with the track meet, it was 99 percent success and only 1 percent failure (we didn't win). Again, it was not winning or losing that was important, but that the school "no one knows" had competed in a city-wide track meet with other larger and well-known schools. Also, when you look over to the bleachers and see our staff and students sitting with what we call "normal" parents, it was something no one ever expected. And then there was the personal stuff: Andrea's father coming to see his daughter compete, and for Andrea, knowing that she could trust that he was going to come and support her with her new choices . . . that was an even bigger deal.

Hours later, Jewels was walking slowly through the Oakland hills until she came to her street and spied the old school mansion that sat alone in the cold darkness.

She was hesitant to return to the school and wake up all the girls because it would mean that there would be all this drama, so she headed over to Mrs. Jackson's house, hoping she might still be up. There were no lights on in the house and she was hesitant to wake Mr. Jackson, so Jewels stood for a few minutes, trying to decide what to do. For the past nine months, she had always had her room at school as a place to return to; her hesitancy made her feel that she was back on the streets again, alone and homeless.

Finally, she walked up to Mrs. Jackson's back door and rang the doorbell. She heard some footsteps inside the house and Louis's barking. Then she could hear Mrs. Jackson talking to herself as she often did when she was upset.

"Now who would be banging on my door at this time of the night?" she mumbled angrily. "Maybe I will call the police."

When Mrs. Jackson finally opened the door, she found Jewels standing motionless in her running suit, a tired expression on her face. Jewels moved quickly toward Mrs. Jackson and embraced her and then began to sob uncontrollably.

"I let them down. I let them down!" she cried. "These girls needed me to be at my best and I let them down."

"Girl, where have you been?" asked Mrs. Jackson, concerned. "You had us all worried sick! One minute you are running around the track and next minute you are gone. You should always stay and shake hands with the winners. It is the polite thing to do. Oh, hush!" scolded Mrs. Jackson to herself. "Always lecturing, sticking my nose in other people's business. I did that once when I came in second in a race that I should have won. You must be hungry and exhausted. Please come in and sit down, and I will make something to eat."

Jewels walked slowly into the kitchen. "You're right. I am sorry. I should never have left without shaking the winners' hands . . . and stayed with the girls. We were a team and we needed to stick together."

"Now we need to eat," explained Mrs. Jackson, pulling out a large pot from the pantry. "My mother always said the best way to get over a defeat is to eat. We used to make chicken gumbo after my meets, although I did not lose very often, but when I did, I was terrible to be around, so we cooked. It relaxed me, and then I would be able to talk about the losing or whatever was on my mind."

Jewels watched Mrs. Jackson get out the ingredients to make chicken gumbo.

While she went about cooking, Jewels remained quiet, watching her cut up the vegetables and adding the different ingredients to what she called the "base."

Jewels sat down at the table. "I am never going back to that school. I mean it. I should have taken the test and left when the going was good."

Mrs. Jackson did not respond and only continued to silently cook.

"I have been trying to help those girls since September," she continued, rubbing her finger on the table's smooth surface as if she were trying to remove the memory of the track meet. "All I got was nothing in return. I am done. I do not care if they send me back to the hall . . . even CYA."

"I used to know a young girl about your age," interrupted Mrs. Jackson with sadness in her voice. "She had all this promise . . . looks, brains, athleticism. She got into the wrong crowd and one night when she was coming home, the driver, who was drinking, hit a tree. Everyone lived except the girl."

Mrs. Jackson stopped and placed her hands over her face and began to cry.

Jewels got up and put her arms around Mrs. Jackson.

"Was that girl your daughter?"

"Yes. I am over it for now. She did not listen to me and I guess you will not listen to me either. I tell you that you got what it takes, girl, but you got to stop thinking about yourself. Those girls need you now and you must step up!"

She stopped talking to let her words hang in the air for a moment, and then she continued, "We are all connected to someone, like this chicken gumbo soup. There can be no gumbo without the chicken. I say you are the chicken and the girls are all the other things you put in. You cannot have one without the other. You are all connected. Your school and those girls are one big gumbo. We cannot survive alone without someone loving and caring about us. So, I say to you, because it is too late, do not go back to your school tonight. Stay the night here and tomorrow I will drive you to take the GED. But remember, you are their leader; yet, without them, you have no school. If you do not go tomorrow, you will all fail. I know you are asking yourself, 'What does some old lady know?' so I will shut my mouth."

"Even if they hate me?" she questioned. "I am not sure if they want me to be with them to take the GED."

"I grew up in the south . . . Alabama," Mrs. Jackson said seriously. "My mama died when I was six, and so it was only papa and me. He was in the service, so we moved around a lot. But there was this time when I was about ten and I had to go to this new school with only a few black kids. Every day at school, they called me names I do not need to repeat. They stole my lunches. They even threw rocks at me. I had no friends. If I had gone to the teacher and snitched, they would have denied it and beaten me up. I never told my father because he, being this military man, would never listen or he would always say, 'When things are bad, you need to suck it up!' It went on for almost a whole year until we moved up here and then I was around more black kids. At night, I often cried into my pillow so my papa would not hear me. I am not telling you what to do, but sometimes you got to suck it up. You may think you are different than those girls, but always remember you are still one of them."

JEWELS ODOM COMMENTARY #54

Anthony always speaks about living history to me and how lucky I am to have Mrs. Jackson in my life and the stories she tells me about her past. For most of us, with the exception of Angel, who always talks about her "grannie," we didn't have families, which means that we have no living history. Hearing her stories about growing up in the South and dealing with prejudice and discrimination gives me a sense of wholeness that I have never had. It is almost like glue that connects the past to the present . . . something all of us need very much, but something the other girls are not getting.

After Mrs. Jackson was finished speaking, Jewels responded, "I so appreciate your sharing your past life with me and I only wish that the rest of the girls can have the chance to hear your stories or at least be around elderly people like you."

"Well," said Mrs. Jackson with a smile, "I think I can help you out. I am involved with a nearby rest home and maybe we can set up a day when your students can come and volunteer to at the rest home and read to the older men and women. They have lots of stories to tell!"

JEWELS ODOM COMMENTARY #55

The old mansion took on a quiet and safe look after dark. During the day everything changed with us girls and our music and dancing, but at night when we slept it was like the old mansion went back to years gone by when there was a neighborhood of families and probably children playing in the street!. Today you rarely see children because most of the expensive homes have replaced the older homes and the people who used to live in those homes have died or their kids have moved away. I guess this is why Mrs. Jackson was so special to me and even to some of the girls, but they never expressed their feelings about her. I just wonder what was going to happen when Mrs. Jackson left for a rest home or even passed away. I often think if I had money I would buy her home and keep her spirit and the spirit of the old neighborhood alive. Maybe I just want to have a past that many of us never had.

THIRTY
GED Tests!

Jamie drove five girls in her car and Anthony seven in the school bus to the GED test site. The only missing student was still Jewels, who had not returned to the school. The police were still out looking for her.

You could hear a pin drop in the car. Even DJ didn't speak, but only looked pensively out of the bus window. Anthony tried to break the silence by talking about the aerobics class when the police had to be called in to break up a riot.

"Shit, looks like Jewels isn't coming," said Patricia, breaking the silence. "She gets to not take the test. Maybe I should have run away after the meet too?"

"Drop it," said Angel. "You got to do what you got to do. Let's just hope she is safe and not with her stupid pimp, Latrell."

"Okay," interrupted Anthony, "remember if you pass one section, you do not need to take it ever again."

"Oh great!" barked DJ. "I really do not need to hear that I will not pass and take the test again."

The girls walked into the testing hall wearing their running suits, and test takers did a double take at the girls all dressed in the same suits that read "Clark Academy." There were even a few thumbs up when they saw Clint's Barbecue on the back of their running suits.

"Hey," whispered Kim, "people are all looking at us like we are a GED testing team. Let's tell them if they help us, we can get them a free meal at Clint's."

"Oh, shut up," said Patricia. "Leave it be. if Jewels wants to do her thing, fine. I am not going to worry about her. It's me first!"

The girls found seats and listened to the proctor about the rules, the GED test, including breaks, and so on. And this would only be the first three test segments. The next test would be the following week.

After a litany of directions, particularly as to how to fill out the test booklet, the proctor said, "Today you will only take the first three mathematics sections. You will have forty-five minutes to take the first test. Then we will take a fifteen-minute break and we will continue with the second mathematics section. Then lunch for an hour and then resume, taking math section number 3. There will not be any talking, and keep your eyes on your own paper. We will pass out pencils. Raise your hand if you need to use the restroom. Any questions?"

No one raised their hands.

"Okay" the proctor continued. "When you get your test, you will—" The tester stopped and looked to the back of the room.

"Excuse me, Miss," she said, peering across the hall to the back entrance. "Are you here for the test?"

Jewels stood in the back of the room dressed in her running outfit and only nodded her head.

"Please come up and sign in," ordered the tester. "We want to start on time."

The Clark Academy girls all turned and viewed Jewels standing alone in the back of the room.

DJ waved and pointed to an empty seat.

Jewels stared straight ahead and walked slowly up to the proctor, signed a form, was given her test, and walked back to an empty seat nearest DJ.

The girls followed Jewels's every move; only Angel refused to make eye contact. Finally, Angel turned and gave a thumbs up to Jewels.

JEWELS ODOM COMMENTARY #56

I know some of the girls got tired the first time they took the real test in math, but we got better with English and the social studies tests.

We would take the tests in the morning, and then return to our afternoon schedule of field trips and so forth. We would get the test results after we completed all the tests, which was good because if we had a really low test score, the girls could freak out and not just refuse to take the tests but bolt from the school and head to the streets and whatever Man on the Floor who would take them in. I would have liked to have taken all the tests over a three- or four-day period, but of course, that would have been suicide for the reason I already explained. Also, the extra time allowed me to work with DJ, who is the weakest of all the girls. I have taken it upon myself to work with her each night for an hour. The challenge is her short attention span. She always finds ways to take breaks and, of course, there is her food issue, which always comes up when she is stressed.

"Food is my medication," she always says. "I just work better when I have something to nibble on."

THIRTY-ONE
I Know She Has Gone to Heaven!

"We should be getting the results back from the junior college in a few days," announced Anthony with a look of trepidation. Then he softened his approach with the comment: "Remember if you pass one section, you never, never have to take it again!"

"And I really, really do not ever want to take the tests again," declared Kim. "Especially when some guy with wicked BO ended up distracting me on the last test."

The girls just looked at each other with expressions like, *Then buy him a can of deodorant!*

"Well," said Tina optimistically, "I know I got my name, date of birth, what school I go to . . . so that should count for something!"

"Okay," continued Anthony. "I have one favor to ask of you all. Our neighbor, Mrs. Jackson, has asked a favor of us and I have agreed."

"She stepped up in several difficult situations," he reminded them. "If you remember, she helped Jewels when she needed to have her dress hemmed and drove Jewels, DJ, and Angel to try and rescue Bonita from the drug dealers."

"She asked us if we would be able to visit the Johnson Rest Home, only a few blocks away, and read to the elders. We have some spare time before GED results are delivered and, of course, dinner and graduation, so let's help the aged!"

"I'll go only if we get lunch," offered DJ, "but no prunes!"

"Those places always smell like when I visited my grannie," said Angel. "I said I would never go back because the place smelled like death and I don't mean Death Valley!"

"Count me out," said Patricia. "I don't need any more death in my life!"

"Excuse me," said Jewels crossly. "Are you forgetting that most of you have been raised by grandmothers or old people because our loser fathers or mothers died and left us to the system?"

"I wouldn't be here if it weren't for my grannie," agreed Angel. "I'm in . . . the rest of you pussies can play that game all you want. I'm goin'."

JEWELS ODOM COMMENTARY #57

It's true. A few of the girls owe their lives to their grannies or older family members who stepped up and saved their behinds when they really needed them! Also, reading to older people at a rest home will be a good reminder about how much our lives have changed from the streets and juvie. Now people are actually trusting us with these old men and women who are so close to death or have been deserted by their families to live out the end of their lives alone. Again, the issues of abandonment always come up with our decision-making, and reading to old people is the least we can do . . . and there is the living history as well.

At approximately 1:30 p.m., the Clark Academy girls appeared in the Johnson Rest Home's large recreation room.

Dianne Clark, the rest home's recreation leader, introduced herself, and then led Anthony and the girls into a large recreation room that was filled with elderly patients. Some were sitting in wheelchairs, others milled around talking, while others were just sleeping.

"I cannot believe that some of these people are still alive.," whispered Angel to Patricia.

"I mean those wheelchairs look like they have cobwebs on them . . . like those in wheelchairs haven't moved in years," returned Patricia.

"Well, maybe if they had a little hooshie, that would wake them up," suggested DJ. "Feed them oysters for about a month. Now that would definitely put lead in all those old guys' pencils."

"Shut up and don't be stupid," whispered Patricia. "They cannot sleep around because they make sure the men sleep with the men and women with women."

"Oh yeah," said Patricia. "Are you talking about birth control or heart attacks?"

"We certainly appreciate you all volunteering to read to our patients," addressed Mrs. Clark.

DJ decided she would rather play cards for jellybeans. But most were paired off to read to various individuals. DJ tried to explain the rules of poker to a fragile black woman named Mrs. Parker but gave up when she realized the woman's hearing aid wasn't working. Instead, they simply played a game of "war."

"High card wins," yelled DJ, flipping over the cards from the top. "The winner is the one that has the most cards after the deck is all used up." Mrs. Parker only smiled and nodded her head in agreement each time she had the higher card.

"Don't get too happy, sister," warned DJ. "Cuz I was cutting you some slack cuz I felt you didn't know how to play!"

"Ahhhhhhhh youth is always wasted on youth," Mrs. Parker uttered with a smile. "I am not as senile as you think. Also, I really like jellybeans!"

Mrs. Clark took Jewels by the arm and led her to where Mrs. Yamamotto, a fragile Japanese woman, was quietly sitting in a nearby corner.

Mrs. Clark whispered to Jewels that the woman couldn't see very well, but her hearing was fine. Then she explained loudly, "This very nice young lady is going to read you a letter from your daughter."

"Hello, my name is Jewels."

Mrs. Yamamotto looked up with a serene smile.

"I think she did not hear you," explained Mrs. Clark. "I think you need to talk louder. Don't be shy."

"Hello!" Jewels said loudly, kneeling down next to the ninety-year-old woman. "I am going to read you a letter from your daughter."

Mrs. Yamamotto clutched Jewels's hand and refused to let go. Then she kissed Jewels's hand and rubbed it against her cheek.

"My dearest mother," read Jewels slowly, "forgive me for not writing sooner, but my work has kept me very busy. I am sorry I could not visit you for Christmas or Easter. Your loving daughter, Monica."

"You read so beautifully," said Mrs. Yamamotto.

"Thanks," replied Jewels, "but I get lots of practice in school."

Jewels looked uncomfortable as the old woman used her hands to explore Jewels's face.

"Your skin is so smooth and your face is full," she said, touching Jewels's face gently. "And you are pretty alright. My hands never lie."

The value of reading to the sick and dying ultimately led to weekly visits by the Clark Academy girls, who took it upon themselves to write letters to the elderly's loved ones. Equally important, this simple act actually remediated the girls' weak writing skills as well as opening up their hearts to the anger they had formed toward their abusive mothers who abandoned them.

JEWELS ODOM COMMENTARY #58

As I read the letter, I become very emotional and had a flashback of an older woman who lived in my foster home who would read to me every night. When the woman became seriously ill, I continued to visit her in the hospital to read to her. One day while I was reading, a nurse appeared to check the old woman's pulse. After taking her pulse, she hurriedly called for a doctor, who appeared and used a stethoscope to listen to the woman's heart.

The doctor and nurse looked at each other, very concerned.

"Little girl," said the doctor, "we think Mrs. Jenson is very tired and it is time for you to return to the lobby with your foster parent."

I ignored the doctor and continued to read.

The nurse began, "I am so sorry but—"

"Don't you understand?" I said seriously. "Every night Mrs. Jenson always read to me and she said someday it would be my turn to read her. I have not finished reading, but I know she is still listening to me. She said she could always hear me even when she's in heaven."

"That's a good girl," said the nurse. "Yes, please, finish the story."

I started to read, but stopped when tears fell on the book's page. I wiped the tears from the page and continued to read for a few more minutes.

The nurse put her arms around me and remained quiet for a time until my foster parent appeared and gave me a hug.

I said to the nurse, "I'm ready to go now. I know she has gone to heaven."

THIRTY-TWO
Pulling for Us to Succeed

Each day like clockwork DJ would wait at her usual spot on the front porch until the postman appeared to deliver the mail. She was waiting for her notification letter of passing or failing the GED tests. There was some weirdness with the testing center and DJ's test scores made her wait while the other girls got their pass or fail grades. Now, all that was left was DJ's. Each day she waited for the mail to appear with her GED grade.

Today, the postman appeared and before he could say a word DJ said, "Thumbs up or thumbs down?"

"Thumbs up," he said with a smile and before he handed her the envelope with her test scores, he gave her a bouquet of flowers.

DJ was stunned by the postman's gesture of kindness and for a change was speechless.

"You've waited so long and you always looked so worried that you didn't pass that I thought the flowers would help you feel better, regardless of your scores," said the postman.

She took a deep breath and said emotionally, "You know I was going to put this letter under my pillow and not open till tomorrow or maybe never, but since you gave me flowers, I owe it to you to open the letter and we can both see my grades."

"Are you sure?" asked the postman. "And by the way my name is John Mayer and I have something else to share with you. When I was about your age, I dropped out of school and got into all sorts of trouble. I got sent to juvenile hall for a few months, and when I got out, I vowed that I would get my high school diploma. Two years later, I finally passed the GED! I didn't pass it on the first time or the second time . . . and I wanted to give up, but I persevered and finally passed it."

"Two times!" yelled DJ. "Holy shit . . . two times!"

DJ opened the letter and she yelled, "I passed everything but English!"

"See?" said John. "You did a lot better than I did on my first time taking the tests. I think I only passed math. Girl you are way ahead of me."

DJ shook his hand and said, "Thank you so much for the flowers. I was so down and afraid I wouldn't pass and your story made me feel so much better. I know I will pass English, and who knows maybe I will become a mailman—or is it mailperson—someday. They sort of go hand in hand."

John left and continued on his route. DJ watched him as he moved through the neighborhood, and she commented, "Yeah, they sort of do go hand in hand, especially if you are a postman."

JEWELS ODOM COMMENTARY #59

We are always surprised by how many people are pulling for us to succeed! Mr. Joseph sometimes stops by to touch base with us, although he makes up excuses like, "I only stopped by to see if you were being nice to the old lady mansion." Then he asks us about our studies and passing the GED. Or, Mrs. Jackson, who got us the gig to read to the old ladies and men at the rest home. And of course, my relationship with Mrs. Jackson can never be ignored. Mr. Chi, who always works with us on the math sections of the GED, is also showing us different ways to stay calm and centered with his breathing exercises. Even the postman stops by if he is ahead of schedule and sits and talks with Mrs. T. about how we are doing.

Funny, but the Man on the Floor cliché started off as very negative and referred to the males who owned and controlled us: the cops, the Louises, pimps, and so forth, but all that has changed. Now when we think of the Man on the Floor, he is not white or black or brown, but only men who we can trust and respect. In my view, this is a huge change in our lives. According to DJ, "You can take that to the bank when you leave the Clark Academy!"

THIRTY-THREE
Two Inches from the Gutter

Anthony promised the girls that if they competed in the track meet, he would take them out for an end-of-the-year lunch "to any restaurant of your choosing." Prior to Anthony's announcement, Chester had made the mistake of volunteering to pay for the meal. Thus, we had two major declarations by Men on the Floor of taking care of these girls; naturally, the girls were going to make sure "they paid for this big time!"

"Any restaurant?" repeated DJ, over and over again, and of course, she was already losing her mind about what meal she would order. "Maybe lobster. Mmmmmmmmm or maybe steak? Not sure what I will have for dessert . . . maybe pie ala modie!"

"It's not 'pie alamodie,' you ingrate," corrected Tina. "It's 'pie a la mode'!"

"It doesn't matter to my stomach," countered DJ. "It just goes in and out all the same."

"You are still an ingrate!"

The girls spent an inordinate amount of time checking all the restaurants in Marin county, especially Sausalito, an upscale town on the water with many expensive seafood restaurants.

"I think I need to run it by Chester," remarked Anthony nervously. "We are talking about some of the most expensive restaurants in the Bay Area, let alone Marin County!"

Angel jumped in, enunciating loudly in Spanish: "*Dijo cualquier restaurante y lo haremos cumplir a usted y a usted*! [He said *any* restaurant and we will hold him to his word!]"

191

She punctuated her remarked with, *"Y puedes llevar eso a cualquier restaurante . . .* and you can take that to your local Taco Bell or wherever! Mr. Cheapskate thinks he's goin' to shortchange us for lunch!"

"Enough of the mumbo jumbo lingo," complained DJ. "Let's get on with where we are goin'. You're making me hungry already!"

"Why not a good Mexican restaurant for lunch?" continued Angel.

"De ninguna manera," countered DJ. "See, I know a little Spanish too!"

"You got something against Mexican food?" asked Angel, getting in DJ's face.

"Last time I heard nobody ever put a whole lobster into a burrrrrrrrrrrrrrito *señorita,"* she defended, walking away.

"For once," uttered Angel, "she might be on to something!"

"And no way are we goin' to Clint's," intervened Kim. "I want to nail Chester with the bill, or as they say on the streets, time to pay up or shut the eff up!"

And so it went until they all agreed that this was a once-in-a-lifetime chance to check out where "rich whities goes for grunts."

The other talk of the week was how they would dress Anthony for the luncheon. Some suggested they rent a tux, others to go drag, while the majority wanted to dress him as a pimp, which, of course, won out.

A few days later Jamie took the girls to a Salvation Army store and the store's clothing pimp selection didn't disappoint. First, they found a bright purple shirt, black pants, a bright green sports jacket with very wide lapels, white shoes with black trim, and, of course, cheap jewelry necklaces.

When Anthony saw the clothing, he pulled back and asked if he could make some modifications to his dress, which, of course, the girls refused.

"Your word is your word," reprimanded Tina, "that's if you don't want me to call in my home boys to slit your tires on your pussy old man car!"

Also, the girls' clothing choices had changed considerably during the year from the black hooker leather pants, black boots, teased hair, and so forth to more classy dresses that Jamie received as donations to the school from high-end SF clothing stores.

When the girls appeared in their new wardrobes, it was like they had just stepped out of a Madison Avenue clothing store.

The day of the luncheon appeared. Anthony waited anxiously on the front porch in his green pimp costume. However, the girls deliberately pretended to ignore him and no one said a word about his attire until DJ couldn't hold back her laughter any further.

"Man, I knew you would be a sorry-looking pimp, but I was wrong; you are even worse than that, even worse than Latrell and that is saying much!"

Seven girls drove with Anthony in his beat-up Saab. Jamie took seven in her car and caravanned over to an upscale Sausalito restaurant. Normally, they would have taken the school bus, but the girls said it would look "tacky" driving into whitie's big shot restaurant in a beat-up yellow school bus. And of course, there was Chester's "pride and joy' Lincoln Continental Mark IV that Chester was reluctantly going to allow Anthony to take for this special occasion.

However, our three amigos (Patricia, Tina, and DJ) decided to take Chester's "pride and joy" for a joy ride one night while Mary had fallen asleep. Never missing a chance for a little fun, they found the car keys and decided to ride around Oakland until DJ got too happy and crashed the Mark IV into several cars and a tree. They abandoned Chester's "pride and joy" and escaped back to school. When Mary realized that the car was gone, and the girls were safely sleeping in their beds, she assumed the car had been stolen. Chester was livid that his "pride and joy" was totaled. He filed a police report, and the "three amigos" got off scot free. Chester met with the entire school to find out if they saw anyone from 9 p.m. or later on the school grounds. Although Chester didn't accuse anyone, you could see it in the girls' faces that something was up.

However, a major problem occurred with Anthony's Saab when he and the girls got to the Richmond–San Rafael Bridge. The Saab's clutch was not the best, which made the trip perilous because they had to drive in the breakdown lane at 35 miles per hour to get over the high bridge grade, while the girls rolled down the windows and pretended to row their way over the bridge, singing "Row, Row, Row Your Boat" to the many strange looks from passing motorists. Finally, a police car appeared and offered to give them special accommodation and led them to the restaurant.

They followed the police car into the restaurant parking lot while several shocked parking attendants looked on in disbelief at the police car, Anthony's old Saab, the young women dressed to the hilt, and finally Anthony, who looked like someone out of another world. The police waved goodbye to the girls, and even Jewels commented that it was really the first time she actually thought a cop was just acting like a person and not a cop.

One attendant sized up the situation and flashed a smile as he watched the fourteen young and very attractive girls walk confidently to "whitie's" restaurant's entrance. The attendant's only remark was to Anthony: "What have you done to deserve this?"

"Karma," said Anthony, "good karma."

The Clark Academy entourage then walked confidently into the restaurant to stares from the predominantly white clientele.

From then on, it was lobster, sirloin steak, and more.

Throughout much of the meal, the waiters spent most of their time talking with the girls about what school they attended, with more looks and comments to Anthony: "You are a very lucky man. No man deserves this!"

"Well," commented Jewels, "I have had many Men on the Floor to deal with, but this is the first time I have ever had waiters on the floor!"

The check came out to about 500 dollars, much to the delight of the girls, because "we are sticking it to Chester!"

They returned to the school and spent the next hour talking about who had had the best meal and, of course, laughed over Anthony's costume.

"Someday I will go back there when I am famous lawyer," remarked DJ. "Really, like you can make a lot of money helping people with food poisoning!"

Finally, Chester never found out who totaled his "pride and joy," regardless that he kept asking the girls, "Are you sure you didn't hear anyone on the school grounds the night my Mark IV was stolen?"

The girls all just shook their heads and left the memory of the Mark IV to perpetuity.

JEWELS ODOM COMMENTARY #60

Whenever we go out into public or especially on whitie's turf, your past as a hoe never leaves you! You always have a fear that someone will recognize you. It is like a scar across your face or when we read that book in English class called "The Red Badge of Courage" that whenever you look in the mirror and see that face or scar, it shoots you right back to the streets. So this day, all I ask is to let us all have a good time, but still when I looked into Anthony's eyes, he knew what I was feeling, but he didn't let on to the girls because it would ruin the day.

THIRTY-FOUR
The Real Game of Life Begins!

A number of guests sat in attendance at the Clark Academy graduation ceremony held at the Oakland, California, Rose Garden: Clark Academy staff, county social workers, psychologists, teachers, parole officers, juvenile hall line staff, school volunteers, local police, Clark Academy students, relatives, and a few street people who were acquainted with the Clark School students. Off to the side stood Mrs. Jackson, Brother Chi, Johnathan Simon, Cecil the barber, Clint of barbecue fame, Andrea's dad, Mr. Joseph, Johnathan Simon, and even John from the San Francisco warehouse.

"Now, I would like to call Jewels Odom to the podium," announced Toni, speaking into a microphone, "to read a poem by Maya Angelou, who, unfortunately, could not personally attend our graduation ceremony, due to a conflict in her schedule. However, Jewels Odom will read Maya Angelou's poem, 'I Know Why the Caged Bird Sings.'"

Jewels walked to the podium and readied herself to read the poem.

Jewels began to speak: "When Maya Angelou was ten years old, she was raped by a man who was a friend of her family."

The microphone let out a loud piercing sound, and Jewels jumped back, nervously cleared her throat, and continued speaking.

"The father asked for the man's name, but Maya hesitated and for a few moments, she was too scared to speak the man's name. Finally, she whispered the man's name, broke down, and cried. The next day, Maya learned that two acquaintances of her father had beaten the man to death. When Maya learned of the man's death, she stopped talking for almost six years because 'my words caused a man's death.' This poem is from her book, *I Know Why the Caged Bird Sings*."

Jewels paused again, took another deep breath, and began to read the poem slowly.

Jewels stopped and wiped a tear from her cheek.

Kim yelled out, "Jewels, we are with you, girl! You rock!"

Jewels blushed and flashed a brief smile and then gave a thumbs up and continued, reading with more determination.

Jewels finished the poem and slowly raised her teary eyes to the crowd. An eerie silence filled the Rose Garden, while the guests waited for Jewels to continue. All eyes were still on Jewels, until DJ stood up and raised her fist and screamed, "You got that right, girl! And you can take that to the Man on the Floor! So go for it, girl! Go for it, girl! You rock, girl!"

Almost on cue, the entire congregation stood up and began to chant, "Jewels! Jewels! Jewels!"

Several homeless graduation crashers joined in the celebration and gave high fives to each other. Jewels flashed an embarrassed wave to the audience, then walked silently back to her seat. Tina ran from her seat and gave Jewels a big hug. Then Mrs. T. embraced Tina and Jewels.

"Girl," said Mrs. T., "you can be on my team any day!"

The Clark School staff and students now huddled around Jewels and took turns giving Jewels hugs and kisses. When she began to cry uncontrollably, it was almost a recognition that her entire ugly past had finally come to a joyous end. All the pain, abuse, and suffering that Jewels and her sister students had experienced in their short lives had become encapsulated into Jewels's reading of the poem and now her tears were tears of joy and truth. In a sense, they were once all caged birds now ready to fly, "for the caged bird sings of freedom!"

Everyone stood up and began to clap in unison. Toni appeared at the podium and gave Jewels a big hug, announcing, "I want everyone to try and make a circle and hold hands while we sing 'The Impossible Dream.'"

Jewels began to sing "The Impossible Dream," and the rest of the audience began to sing with her.

After they finished singing, Toni and Chester gave out the GED certificates of completion.

Toni announced: "The three students who passed the GED 100% are Jewels Odom, Angel Rivera, and Andrea Parker. Please come up for your certificates."

Chester announced, "The students who completed other parts of the GED, please come up when you hear you name."

"Patrician Green!"

"Kim Chambers!"

"DJ Thomas!"

"Charlene Olsen!"

"Tanya Tennyson!"

"Jacqueline Majors!"

"Madeline Olsen!"

"Maria Ochoa!"

"Shamitta Rice!"

"Shannon Jones!"

"Candice Johnson!"

"Congratulations to all our students!" yelled Toni. "And you can take that to next time you finish your GED!"

"Guests who wish to celebrate, please come to the Clark School Academy from 2 p.m. to 5 p.m. today for refreshments. Thank you."

Toni turned the microphone over to Chester, and for a moment, he was speechless, and then he passed the microphone to Mrs. T., who yelled, "And you can take that to the diploma Man on the Floor!"

JEWELS ODOM COMMENTARY #61

Ok, so here we or I am standing alone just like I use to stand on the Oakland streets selling my body. It was weird that instead it was my brain that was speaking and the Men on the Floor were looking at me with respect, someone with a brain who was going to do something more in life. Then I start thinking about these girls and what might happen to them. Is this like a one-shot deal or like a "throw or a blow"?

Epilogue

The Circle of Life!

Anthony was walking up a tree-lined path on a Northern California university campus. Students hurried past to classes, while others mingled around, talking with each other or studying. Anthony walked slowly, going over in his mind his lecture for his child development class. He had an academic look that included a brown herringbone jacket, black turtleneck, and black pants. His beard was trimmed neatly, and his black hair was combed back. He walked past the university sports field and heard the public address announce the names of the runners in the 800-meter track competition, until he heard "in lane 2, Jewels Odom!"

Anthony froze in his tracks and tried to comprehend what he had just heard over the loudspeaker. He shook his head as if to shake out the cobwebs and silently asked himself, *Did I hear what I think I heard?*

He rushed over to the fence that enclosed the track and peered through to get a better view of the runners, but the starting point was too far away for him to make out if the runner was truly Jewels who was truly in college and running in the track meet. He heard the starter's pistol fire and the shouts from the crowd. He strained to see the runners, who would be closing in on the finish line nearest to where Anthony was peering through the fence. When the runners raced by the fence, he recognized the lead runner as Jewels. She was more muscular and her hair shorter, but it was clearly Jewels. When the race ended, Anthony rushed over to an entrance that led to the track and walked slowly over to where Jewels was standing with several other runners. She reached down to pick up a water bottle.

"Go easy on the water," said Anthony. "You do not want to get cramps."

She raised her head to the voice, and when she saw Anthony, she was speechless. She rushed over to him, giving him a big hug, and for a period of time, both were silent.

"I'm shocked," she said, wiping a tear from her cheek. "I can't believe it's actually you! It was like you disappeared and no one knew what happened to you. I have thought about you often."

"How long has it been? Four years?" asked Anthony, trying to compose himself. "We need to talk. Can we go over to some place quiet to talk?"

They walked, finding a quiet corner under the grandstands.

"You disappeared after we were emancipated," continued Jewels. "Then I went to the JC and ran track and got my AA in early childhood education, and finally transferred to the university."

"Where have you been living?" asked Anthony.

Jewels became quiet and dropped her head, remaining quiet until she broke down and started crying, "I'm sorry. I'm so sorry."

"What?" asked Anthony, concerned.

"I stayed with Mrs. Jackson for two years while at the JC and then . . . well . . ." Jewels took a breath, trying to control her emotions, "she had a heart attack and passed away." Jewels started crying. "She was like the grandmother and mother I never had. It has been really hard without her."

Anthony remained quiet and listened to Jewels.

"In her will, she said that once her house was sold, all the money would go into a trust fund in my name. It would pay for my room and board, college fees. Then, I got this scholarship for track. She was such a wise, caring woman. She always said that she would start me off in the race of life. I guess I am a strong finisher."

Anthony and Jewels sat in the grandstands and talked until Anthony said, "Oh my God, I have a class to teach!"

"Give me your phone number, and I will call you and we can have lunch," said Jewels.

"We have lots to talk about, Mr. Man on the Floor from the Harvard Project!"

JEWELS ODOM COMMENTARY #62

Anthony would always talk about life being like a circle that you could end up where you begin. Talking with Anthony brought this idea back to me as I sat and looked at him and wondered where we all would be if he hadn't shown up at our school to do the pizza lesson that stressed us out, like, "Here we go again. We got to pass the GED and get emancipated, and this Harvard guy is teaching us how to make freakin' pizza!" He realized if we were ever going to trust our real intelligence, we needed to move from our street smarts to school smarts. I mean, that is what he repeated over and over again until it finally stuck, and like, the circle was here again when I was trying to convince him that he was a different Man on the Floor!

THE END

About the Author

David P. Sortino (EdM, PhD) holds a master's degree in human development from Harvard University and a doctorate in clinical psychology from Saybrook University. In addition, Dr. Sortino possesses multiple subject learning-handicap and resource-specialist teaching credentials.

Over the last forty years, he has served as a director and principal to several residential school programs for learning-handicap and seriously emotionally disturbed students in public and private education at the elementary, middle, and secondary school levels. Moreover, he has served as a moral-development consultant to state and county programs for at-risk youth (juvenile hall) and currently works directly with individuals and families as an educational consultant and neurofeedback practitioner.

In his private practice, Dr. Sortino consults and collaborates with students, parents, teachers, and psychologists to provide support for students in pre-K through college in establishing school success and higher learning levels. He finds that exploring how the brain learns, as well as other learning strategies, can help students develop a better understanding of their learning potential in and out of the classroom.

Presently, he directs the Neurofeedback Institute, writes a blog for the *Santa Rosa Press Democrat*, and hosts a bimonthly radio show called "Brain Smart: A Better Learning Brain" on KOWS, 98.7 FM. He is the author of *The Promised Cookie: No Longer Angry Children* (2011—Author House), *A Guide to How Your Child Learns: Understanding the Brain from Early Childhood to Young Adulthood* (2018—Rowman and Littlefield), *Brain Changers: Major Advances in Children's Learning and Intelligence* (2019—Rowman and Littlefield), and *Brain Gains: So, You Want to Be Your Child's Learning Coach?* (2020—Rowman and Littlefield). He is married and the father of two daughters: Abby and Shai.